Questions on the Lord's Supper

Rev. Joshua Sullivan

DEDICATION

To the Saints at Holy Cross Lutheran Church in Kerrville, Texas

CONTENTS

viii

Introduction

Whether it is called the Lord's Supper, the Sacrament of the Altar, the Lord's Table, or the Eucharist, the meal that Christ instituted on the night in which He was betrayed is central to the life of the church and the Christian.

It is also a source of significant disagreement among Christians. Some think the bread and wine are symbols of Christ's body and blood. Others think Christ is bodily present in the elements of bread and wine. Still others think Christ's presence is only a spiritual presence. For those who believe Christ is bodily present in the Sacrament, they disagree on the mechanics of how He is present. Rome teaches the substances of bread and wine are transformed into Christ's real body and blood. Others teach the bread and wine remain and Christ's body and blood are enclosed within the bread and wine. Others believe simply the elements remain while Christ is present with His body and blood in a supernatural way.

There is also disagreement as to the purpose of the Lord's Supper and its practice. Who can administer the Sacrament? What elements are allowable? Can it be enclosed in a tabernacle? Can Christians celebrate the Lord's Supper over the internet?

Lutherans have traditionally answered nearly every question about the Sacrament from Christ's *words of institution*, the words in Matthew, Mark, Luke, and 1 Corinthians in which Jesus takes bread and wine, blesses and distributes them to the disciples to eat and drink. So much of the confusion and disagreement over the Sacrament can be removed if we read the plain words of Christ and take them at face value. It is my hope that this volume does just that.

The Lutheran Confessions are frequently used. Lutherans do not view these documents as equal to Scripture. Rather, they are a true confession and exhibition of what Scripture teaches. All citations from the Lutheran Confessions are from the Henkel translation of the Book of Concord, second edition (Newmarket: S.D. Henkel, 1854).

Abbreviations for Lutheran Confessional Documents:

AC – Augsburg Confession

AP - Apology of the Augsburg Confession

SC - Small Catechism

LC - Large Catechism

SA – Smalcald Articles

Tr – Treatise on the Power and Primacy of the Pope

FC Epitome – Formula of Concord, Epitome

FC SD - Formula of Concord, Solid Declaration

Quotations from Martin Luther works are taken from Luther's Works, American Edition, vols. 1–30, ed. Jaroslav Pelikan (St. Louis: Concordia, 1955–76); vols. 31–55, ed. Helmut Lehmann (Philadelphia/Minneapolis: Muhlenberg/Fortress, 1957–86), hereafter AE in the footnotes.

Christ's Real Presence in the Sacrament

Q: The passage for the Real Presence doctrine reads: "And he took bread, and gave thanks, and brake it, and gave unto them, saying, 'This is my body which is given for you: this do in remembrance of me.'" Do this in remembrance. This word is the significant word as if you are remembering him, it is because you are believing in him and his sacrifice which corresponds with Sola Fide. The Lord's Supper was actually the Passover of Jesus where Jesus was the sacrificial lamb. "I am the good shepherd." "I am the vine." These are symbolic just as He is symbolically saying this is my body speaking about physical sacrifice while the communion is symbolic of that physical sacrifice.

A: Lutherans believe in the real presence of Christ in the Lord's Supper. By "real presence" we mean that Christ is bodily, substantially present in, with, and under the bread and wine. The bread is the true body of Christ while simultaneously remaining bread. The wine is His true blood while simultaneously remaining wine. This is not transubstantiation—as will be demonstrated in a later chapter—nor is it consubstantiation. Lutherans hear Jesus' words, 'This is my body; This is my blood," and believe that to be true.

Lutherans call those who deny the bodily presence of Christ in the Sacrament *Sacramentarians*, of which there are two types.

Some are gross sacramentarians, who, as indeed they believe in their hearts, allege in clear and explicit words, that in the Lord's Supper, nothing more than bread and wine are present, administered, and received with the lips. But others are artful and the most pernicious of all sacramentarians ; these in part use our words most speciously, and pretend that they also believe a real presence of the true, essential, or substantial, body and blood of Christ in the holy sacrament of the Lord's Supper ; yet they maintain, that this comes to pass spiritually, through faith. Now, under these specious words they conceal the gross opinion of the former class, namely, that in the Lord's Supper, there is nothing present, and received with the lips, beside the bread and wine. (Epitome VII.3-5)

Gross Sacramentarians deny Christ's bodily presence and confess that only bread and wine are present in the Lord's Supper. The bread and wine are merely symbols of Christ's true body and blood. The arguments presented above are the two standard arguments for the symbolic understanding of the Lord's Supper.

The first argument against Christ's real presence in the Supper is the interpretation of Christ's words, "This do in remembrance of me." The Sacramentarians read these words to mean that when we eat and drink the bread and wine, we simply call to mind Christ's innocent, bitter sufferings and death and think of His sacrifice for our sins. This understanding of "Do this in remembrance of Me" makes the Lord's Supper just another proclamation of the Gospel. It is a proclamation of the Gospel, but it's much more than that. To "do this in remembrance of me" means to remember Christ's sacrifice *and* receive the benefits of His sacrifice by faith. Lutherans confess in the *Apology of the Augsburg Confession*:

> The doing of this, in remembrance of Christ, does not consist merely in external acts, performed merely as an admonition and example, as in history, we remember the deeds of Alexander and others ; but it means to know Christ truly, seeking and desiring his benefits. Now the faith which perceives the abounding grace of God, is life-giving. This is the principal use of the Sacrament, from which it readily appears who are really prepared to

receive it, namely, those who are alarmed, who feel their sins, dread the wrath and judgment of God, and long for consolation. The Psalmist, therefore, says : "He hath made his wonderful works to be remembered : the Lord is gracious and full of compassion. He hath given meat unto them that fear him," Psalm 111:4–5. The faith which acknowledges this mercy, gives life to the soul ; and this is the proper use of the Sacrament. (Ap XXIV.72-73)

When we faithfully eat of Christ's body and blood in the Sacrament, we are remembering Christ's sufferings and death but in such a way that we receive the benefits He earned in by His suffering and death: the forgiveness of sins, life, and salvation. It is not simply something we do to remember Christ's death. Because the bread is the body of Christ and the wine is His true blood, He bestows on us the benefits of His cross: the forgiveness that He earned for us there.

The second argument against Christ's real presence in the Sacrament deals with the interpretation of the word "is." Lutherans, along with the church fathers, read the *words of institution* literally according to their plain sense. Is means is. Sacramentarians claim that Christ's words are obscure. Some claim the word "this" refers to Christ's physical body sitting at the table that night. Others imagine the pronoun "this" refers to the bread and wine, but by "is" Jesus means "represents," "signifies," or "symbolizes." This makes the word of Christ obscure because He uses the word "is" but He means something else entirely. The assumption is that since Jesus uses figures of speech elsewhere in the gospels He must be speaking figuratively when He instituted the Sacrament.

How are such bold assertions to be answered? Three things can be said in defense of a literal reading of the *words of institution*. First, the Lord's Supper is an article of faith with serious consequences for those who eat and drink unworthily, as Paul says in 1 Corinthians 11:29. Since it is an article of faith it has to be explained clearly. The *words of institution* recorded by Matthew, Mark, Luke and Paul, are the *sedes doctrinae*, or the 'seat of doctrine,' the place in Scripture where Christ tells us plainly what we are to believe about the Sacrament.

Second, Christ gives the Lord's Supper to His church as His testament, as in the last will and testament of a dying man. In Galatians 3:15 Paul says of a man-made testament, "Though it is only a man's covenant, yet if it is confirmed, no one annuls or adds to it." When a last will and testament is executed, it must be done by the letter. Figurative or symbolic language isn't allowed in one's last will and testament. Since it is the final wishes of the testator it is written in plain speech to avoid ambiguity and misunderstanding. The will must be executed according to the letter. The executor must stick to the actual words.

Third, when Jesus says, "I am the vine," "I am the door," or, "I am the Good Shepherd," He's not saying that He symbolizes the vine, the door, and the Good Shepherd. That's what He would be saying if we took the verb "am" as Sacramentarians want to take "is" in the *words of institution*. The figure isn't the verb "is." The figure is in the predicate, the object of the verb "is." Johann Gerhard says this about Jesus being the true vine: "This can by no means be interpreted that Christ symbolizes a wine-stalk (vine), because the text here speaks not of an earthly vine, but of the true, that is, of the spiritual, heavenly Wine-Stalk, onto which the apostle and all believers are engrafted as tendril shoots. That very same true, spiritual Wine-Stalk does not symbolize Christ; rather He Himself is it."[1] When Christ says He

---

[1] Johann Gerhard, *Comprehensive Explanation of Holy Baptism and the Lord's Supper (1610)*, trans. Elmer Hohle (Malone, TX: Repristination Press, 2014), 289.

is the door, He does not mean that He signifies a door, or that He is an ordinary door. He says, "I am the door. If anyone enters by Me, he will be saved" (John 10:9). He is the spiritual door by which people enter God's kingdom. In all of these and the other examples, "is" still means "is." The figure is in the predicate, not the verb. The same is true when Paul calls Christ "our Passover" (1 Corinthians 5:7) and the "spiritual rock" from which Israel drank and followed them in the wilderness (1 Corinthians 10:4). Christ doesn't symbolize the Passover or the rock. He is the Passover and the spiritual rock which followed Israel in the wilderness.

We also have the proper understanding of Christ's words taught by St. Paul. He writes in 1 Corinthians 10:16, "The cup of blessing which we bless, is it not the communion of the blood of Christ? The bread which we break, is it not the communion of the body of Christ?" St. Paul is as clear as Christ. The cup of blessing is communion with the blood of Christ, just as the bread is the communion, or participating in, Christ's very body. If Christ isn't bodily present in the Sacrament then it would not be a communion with His body, but a communion only of the spirit of Christ. Paul's word here, along with 1 Corinthians 11, show that Paul himself did not take Christ's words figuratively but literally.

Closely related, though slightly different from this, is the *Subtle Sacramentarian* position. *Subtle Sacramentarians* are generally the followers of the Swiss Reformer John Calvin such as Presbyterians. They deny the bread and wine are empty symbols as the *Gross* Sacramentarians. They believe in a real spiritual presence of Christ in the Sacrament but deny His bodily presence. For Calvin, the bread and wine are symbols by which the thing signified—that is, Christ—is also shown. Calvin wrote, "And the godly ought by all means to keep this rule: whenever they see symbols appointed by the Lord, to think and be persuaded that the truth of the thing signified is surely present there."[2] Although Calvin can speak of Christ's presence and benefits in the Sacrament, it is a spiritual rather than bodily presence.

One of Calvin's main objections to Christ's bodily presence in the Sacrament is his assumption that Christ's human body is just like ours and does not receive divine majesty from its union with the divine nature. He writes, "For as we do not doubt that Christ's body is limited by the general characteristics common to all human bodies, and is contained in heaven (where it was once for all received) until Christ return in judgment [Acts 3:21], so we deem it utterly unlawful to draw it back under these corruptible elements or to imagine it to be presence everywhere."[3] He writes elsewhere that "we must establish such a presence of Christ in the Supper as may neither fasten him to the element of bread, nor enclose him in bread, nor circumscribe him in any way (all things which things, it is clear, detract from his heavenly glory); finally such as many not take from him his own stature, or parcel him out to many places at once, or invest him with boundless magnitude to be spread through heaven and earth. For these are plainly in conflict with a nature truly human."[4]

Calvin works, not from the *words of institution*, as much as what it means to have a truly human nature. He assumes that since Christ's human nature is the same ours, excepting sin, and we cannot be in more than one place at a time, neither can Jesus' body be present anywhere else than in heaven which contains Him. Calvin denies that Christ's divine nature shares its divine

---

[2] John Calvin, *Institutes of the Christian Religion*, Library of Christian Classics, ed. John T. McNeill, trans. F. L. Battles, 2 vols. (Philadelphia: Westminster, 1960), 1:1371 (4.17.10)

[3] Ibid., 1373 (4.17.12)

[4] Ibid., 1381 (4.17.19)

power and majesty with the human nature of Christ, so that the human nature is capable of things beyond its natural properties. By stating that Christ's glory would be diminished if His presence was fastened or circumscribed to the bread and wine, Calvin assumes He knows better than God what suits His glory. Against these ideas, Lutherans "give Christ this honor, that, by the power of His promise, He is able to give us His body and blood in the Super while leaving intact the integrity of His human nature, although how He does or is able to do this we are not able to discover."[5]

There is nothing about the context of the *words of institution* which lead us to read them symbolically or figuratively. Only the belief that human reason must be able to comprehend what God gives us leads to that conclusion. Sacramentarians, both gross and subtle, view Christ's *words of institution* figuratively when there is no textual warrant to do so. Instead, they ought to be read according to their plain sense and believed in faith.

---

[5] Johann Gerhard, *Succinct and Select Theoogical Aphorisms*, trans. Paul Rydecki (Malone, TX: Repristination Press, 2018), 157.

Are Sins Forgiven in Holy Communion?

Q: By partaking of Holy Communion are our sins forgiven?

A: What's the purpose of Holy Communion? Why did Christ give His Christians His body and blood to eat and drink? The answer lies in Christ's words by which He instituted the Sacrament because in the institution He tells us not only *what* the Lord's Supper is, but what its *purpose* is. The *words of institution* are recorded in Matthew, Mark, Luke, and 1 Corinthians. For our purposes let's look at St. Paul's and St. Matthew's account. The Evangelist writes in 26:26-28,

> Jesus took bread, and blessed it, and brake it, and gave it to the disciples, and said, 'Take, eat; this is my body.' And he took the cup, and gave thanks, and gave it to them, saying, 'Drink ye all of it; For this is my blood of the new testament, which is shed for many for the remission of sins.'

Jesus specially says of the cup—by which He means the wine in the cup,—"This is my blood of the new testament, which is shed for many for the forgiveness of sins." That last phrase is the answer to the question. What is the purpose of the Lord's Supper? To forgive—or remit—sins.

Luther teaches in the *Small Catechism*: "What is the benefit of such eating and drinking? Answer: That is shown us in these words: Given, and shed for you, for the remission of sins; namely, that in the Sacrament forgiveness of sins, life, and salvation are given us through these words. For where there is forgiveness of sins, there is also life and salvation." The purpose of partaking of the Sacrament of Christ's true body and blood is to receive the forgiveness of sins which Christ won for us by His innocent, bitter sufferings and death upon the cross. Luther then asks:

How can bodily eating and drinking do such great things? Answer: It is not the eating and drinking, indeed, that does them, but the words which stand here, namely: Given, and shed for you, for the remission of sins. Which words are, beside the bodily eating and drinking, as the chief thing in the Sacrament; and he that believes these words has what they say and express, namely, the forgiveness of sins.

Christ instituted His Sacrament to bestow the forgiveness of sins, life, and salvation upon those who partake of the Sacrament in faith, since faith receives what is being offered. The worthy communicant receives Christ's true body and blood in, with, and under the forms of bread and wine. The worthy communicant also receives, through Christ's body and blood, the forgiveness of sins, and with forgiveness comes life and salvation.

Forgiveness of sins is never by itself. Where Christ forgives sins He gives new life, His own divine life, so that we may walk by the Spirit, forsaking sins and pursuing righteousness. The fathers of the church regularly confessed that the Lord's Supper bestows these blessings on the one who partakes worthily. Ignatius of Antioch (d. 110) describes the Lord's Supper as "the medicine of immortality, the antidote we take in order not to die but to live forever in Jesus Christ."[6]

Ambrose of Milan (ca.339-397) writes in his treatise entitled *On the Sacraments*, "He who ate manna died; but he who has eaten this body, it will become for him the forgiveness of sins and he 'shall not die forever.'[7] He writes later in the same work, "I

---

[6] All translations of Ignatius of Antioch are taken from Michael Holmes, *The Apostolic Fathers: Greek Texts and English Translations*, 3rd Edition (Grand Rapids, MI: Baker Academic, 2007).

[7] Book IV.24 in Daniel J. Sheerin, The Eucharist, Vol. 7, Message of the Fathers of the Church (Wilmington, DE: Michael Glazier, 1986), 80.

ought always to receive Him, that He may always forgive my sins. I, who sin always, should have a medicine always."[8]

Cyril of Alexandria (d. 444) writes something similar in his *Commentary on John*. He writes that "since the flesh of the Savior has become life-giving (in that it has been united to that which is by nature life, namely, the Word from God), when we taste of it, then we have life in ourselves, since we too are united to that flesh just as it is united to the Word who indwells it."[9] He writes later that by eating Christ's body and drinking His blood by faith, "Christ implants his own life into the faithful by their participation in his flesh, according to the statement, "Whoever eats my flesh and drinks my blood has eternal life."[10] He notes elsewhere that we aren't only united with Christ spiritually, but bodily as well. He writes:

> Now the substance of our doctrine will in no way deny that we are united spiritually with Christ by a disposition of perfect love, by a right and uncorrupted faith, and by a virtuous and pure mind. We agree that he is quite right in saying this. But we will show that the bold claim that there is no reference to a union according to the flesh between us and him is completely out of harmony with the divine Scriptures. How could there be any dispute, and what right-thinking person could ever doubt that Christ is the vine in this sense? And we, filling the role of branches, take into ourselves the life that comes out of and from him. . . Let anyone interpret this for us and teach us what it means without reference to the power of

---

[8] Ibid., 81. (Book IV.26)

[9] Cyril of Alexandria. *Commentary on John*. Edited by Joel Elowsky. Translated by David Maxwell. Vol. 1. Ancient Christian Texts. Downers Grove, IL: IVP Academic, 2013), 236.

[10] Cyril of Alexandria. *Commentary on John*. Edited by Joel Elowsky. Translated by David Maxwell. Vol. 2. Ancient Christian Texts. Downers Grove, IL: IVP Academic, 2015), 76.

the mystical blessing [the Lord's Supper]. Why do we receive it without ourselves? Does it not make Christ dwell in us bodily by participation and communion with his holy flesh? . . . By the participation in the body of Christ and his precious blood, we are united so that he is in us, and we are in him. There was no other way that what was subject to decay by nature could be made alive except by being combined bodily with the body of him who is life by nature, that is, the Only begotten.[11]

Since Christ's human flesh is united to God the Word, it is life-giving flesh. Since He gives us His very flesh and blood in the Lord's Supper, He unites with believers physically as well as spiritually, putting His divine life and immortality in them so that it may spring up into everlasting life at the resurrection of all flesh on the Last Day. These words from Ignatius in the first century, Ambrose in the fourth, and Cyril in the fifth show that the church has always trusted Christ to give His life-giving flesh and blood to the worthy communicant for the forgiveness of sins, life, and salvation.

What makes a communicant worthy? Worthiness does not consist of perfect, for that is impossible in this life, nor does it consist of not being aware of any sins in one's conscience. Cyril of Alexandria writes:

When then will you be worthy? We will reply to whoever says this. When will you present yourself to Christ? If you are always going to be frightened by your stumbling—and you will never stop stumbling (since, "who can understand their errors?" as the holy psalmist says)—you will be found completely without participation in the saving sanctification. Therefore, you should decide to live a more reverent life in accordance with the law and so

---

[11] Ibid, 214.

participate in the blessing, believing it to drive away not only death but also our diseases. When Christ has come to be in us, he puts to sleep the law which rages in the members of our flesh. He kindles reverence toward God and deadens our passions, not counting against us the transgressions we are in but rather healing us as people who are ill. He binds out what has been crushed, he raises what has fallen, and he does this as the good shepherd who has laid down his life for the sheep.[12]

Being worthy means that one is contrite over one's sins, trusting that by His body and blood He forgives your sin, and you strive to amend your sinful life by the power of the Holy Spirit. Lutherans confess in the *Formula of Concord*:

But the worthy guests are Christians, weak indeed in faith, fainthearted and afflicted, who, on account of the magnitude and the multitude of their sins, are alarmed in their hearts, who, in view of their great impurity, judge themselves unworthy of this noble treasure and of the benefits of Christ, who feel and deplore their weakness of faith, and desire from their hearts to be able to serve God with a stronger, and more joyful faith, and with pure obedience ; these are the truly worthy guests, for whom this most august sacrament was chiefly instituted and ordained. For thus Christ most benignly invites every one, saying : "Come unto me, all ye that labor and are heavy laden, and I will give you rest," Matt. 11:28. Again, "They that be whole need need not a physician, but they that are sick," Matt. 9:12. Again, "My strength is made perfect in weakness," 2 Cor. 12:9. Again, "Him that is weak in the faith, receive ye ;—for God hath received him," Rom. 14:1,3. "For whosoever believeth in the Son of God," be it with a weak or strong faith, "hath everlasting life," John

---

[12] Cyril of Alexandria. *Commentary on John*. Vol. 1, 239.

3:16 (FC SD VII:69-70).

This means the unworthy communicant is the one who refuses to acknowledge their sin, does not seek the forgiveness of sins, does not want to amend their sinful life, or disbelieves Christ's words. St. Paul writes in 1 Corinthians 11:27-29, "Therefore whoever eats this bread or drinks this cup of the Lord in an unworthy manner will be guilty of the body and blood of the Lord. But let a man examine himself, and so let him eat of the bread and drink of the cup. For he who eats and drinks in an unworthy manner eats and drinks judgment to himself, not discerning the Lord's body." The unworthy communicant receives the essence of the Sacrament—Christ's true body and blood—but not the benefit of the Sacrament—forgiveness of sins, life, and salvation. The bread and wine are not simultaneously Christ's body and blood only for the believing since God's Word effects Christ's sacramental presence. Lutherans confess in the *Formula of Concord* that

> such persons receive it unto judgment, as St. Paul, 1 Cor. 11:29, declares ; for they misuse this holy sacrament, because they receive it without true repentance and without faith. For it was instituted for the purpose of testifying, that unto those the grace and benefits of Christ are here appropriated, and that those are united with Christ and cleansed by his blood, who truly repent and console themselves through faith in Christ. (FC SD VII.16)

The communicant who refuses to repent of his or her sins mocks the Lord's purpose in giving the Sacrament. Those who refuse to believe that the bread is truly Christ's body and the wine is truly Christ's blood eat and drink condemnation on themselves because they do not discern the Lord's body. Some want to make "the body" that should be discerned "the church" since the church is often called the body of Christ, but Paul is not talking about recognizing the church as Christ's body. If one eats and drinks without faith, without believing that the bread is Christ's true body and that the wine is Christ's true blood, then that one does not receive the forgiveness of sins, but receives Christ's true body and blood to their judgment and condemnation. Luther summarizes this well in the *Small Catechism* when he asks, "Who then receives the Sacrament worthily?"

> Fasting and keeping the body in subjection, are indeed a good external discipline ; nevertheless, he only is truly worthy, and well prepared, who has faith in these words : *"given and shed for you, for the remission of sins."* But he who disbelieves these words, or doubts, is unworthy and unprepared ; since the expression *"for you"* requires only such hearts as believe.

Forgiveness of sins is offered in the Lord's Supper, along with Christ's true body and true blood, and believing Christians receive just that. He who partakes of the supper unworthily, without repentance or faith that Christ is bodily present, does not have his sins forgiven but drinks judgment upon himself according to the words of the Holy Spirit through St. Paul. This should admonish all Christians to examine themselves properly before coming to the Lord's Supper, acknowledging their sin and their sinful nature, and trusting that Christ, through His body and blood, wants to forgive our sins, give us His life, and promise us eternal salvation.

Transubstantiation

Q: Do Lutherans believe in transubstantiation?

A: Lutherans reject transubstantiation. Before we explore why, it will be helpful to clarify Rome's doctrine. The Roman Catholic Catechism explains:

> The Council of Trent summarizes the Catholic faith by declaring: "Because Christ our Redeemer said that it was truly his body that he was offering under the species of bread, it has always been the conviction of the Church of God, and this holy Council now declares again, that by the consecration of the bread and wine there takes place a change of the whole substance of the bread into the substance of the body of Christ our Lord and of the whole substance of the wine into the substance of his blood. This change the holy Catholic Church has fittingly and properly called transubstantiation."[13]

The word transubstantiation means "change of substance." According to the Council of Trent, when a priest consecrates the elements of bread and wine there is a change of substance. The whole substance of bread is changed into the body of Christ. The whole substance of wine is changed into Christ's blood. Yet both retain their incidental properties. The elements retain the form of bread and wine, which means they still look like, feel like, smell like, and taste like bread and wine, but the bread is no longer bread and the wine is no longer wine.

The problem with transubstantiation is that it isn't Scriptural. It's a philosophical explanation of Christ's real presence that goes beyond Scripture and contradicts Scriptures. Christ's *words of institution* don't teach a change of substance. He doesn't say that this bread is no longer bread, but that it is His body and

---

[13] Catechism of the Catholic Church, 1376

that the wine is His blood. He speaks of a union of two natures, one earthly, the other heavenly.

St. Paul call the consecrated bread "bread" before **and after** the consecration. He writes in 1 Corinthians 11:26-28, "For as often as you eat this bread and drink this cup, you proclaim the Lord's death till He comes. Therefore whoever eats this bread or drinks this cup of the Lord in an unworthy manner will be guilty of the body and blood of the Lord." He also writes in 1 Corinthians 10:16, "The cup of blessing which we bless, is it not the communion of the blood of Christ? The bread which we break, is it not the communion of the body of Christ?" Johann Gerhard observes, "For, if a thing is changed into something else, then one cannot say that one is the fellowship of the other."[14] The bread, not just the outward appearance of the bread, is the fellowship with Christ's body.

The Lutheran Reformers confessed that the expressions "under the bread, with the bread, in the bread, have been used for the purpose of rejecting the Popish doctrine of transubstantiation, and for the purpose of indicating the sacramental union of the unchanged essence of the bread and of the body of Christ" (FC SD VII:35). This sacramental union of the bread and Christ's body, of the wine and Christ's blood, is similar to the personal union of the human and divine natures in Christ. When "The Word became flesh" the divine essence wasn't changed into the human nature. Two unchanged natures, human and divine, are personally united. They confessed in the *Formula of Concord*:

> And indeed, many eminent ancient teachers, Justin, Cyprian, Augustine, Leo, Gelasius, Chrysostom, and others, employ even this similitude (concerning the person of Christ) in explaining the words of the testament of Christ, "This is my body." For they teach that, as in

---

[14] Gerhard, *Comprehensive Explanation*, 301.

Christ, there are two different, unchanged natures united inseparably, so in the holy sacrament of the Lord's Supper, the two substances, the natural bread, and the true natural body of Christ, are together present here on earth in the instituted administration of this sacrament. Yet this union of the body and blood of Christ with the bread and the wine, is not a personal union like that of the two natures in Christ, but it is a sacramental union (FC SD VII:36).

Scripture clearly teaches that the bread and wine remain bread and wine even as the human nature the Son of God assumed remained a complete and true human nature. Practically speaking, this means after the consecration the bread is still bread, but it is also the real body of Christ. The wine is still wine but it is simultaneously the true blood of Christ.

The Lutheran reformers also show Trent's words as false when the council stated that transubstantiation "has always been the conviction of the Church of God." The council cites several early church witnesses to the sacramental union, not a transubstantiation. Justin Martyr (d. 155 A.D.) compares the Eucharist to the incarnation of our Lord Jesus Christ. He writes in his *First Apology*:

> Not as ordinary bread or as ordinary drink do we partake of them, but just as, through the word of God, our Savior Jesus Christ became Incarnate and took upon Himself flesh and blood for our salvation, so, we have been taught the food which has been made the Eucharist by the prayer of His word, and which nourishes our flesh and blood by assimilation, is both the flesh and blood of that Jesus who was made flesh.[15]

---

[15] Fathers of The Church, *Saint Justin Marytr*, trans. Thomas B. Falls, (New York: Christian Heritage, Inc., 1948), p.105-106

Irenaeus of Lyon (d. 185 A.D.) describes the Eucharist as consisting of two realities, not just one reality with the incidental properties of another reality. He writes in *Against Heresies*,

> For as the bread, which is produced from the earth, when it receives the invocation of God, is no longer common bread,but the Eucharist, consisting of two realities, earthly and heavenly; so also our bodies, when they receive the Eucharist, are no longer corruptible, having the hope of the resurrection to eternity.[16]

Gelasisus, Bishop of Rome (ca. 490 A.D.) wrote, "By the sacraments we are made partakers of the divine nature, and yet the substance and nature of bread and wine do not cease to be in them."[17] Trent's claim that transubstantiation has always been the church's conviction isn't true. In reality, the doctrine came from scholastic theologians of the middle ages, which is why transubstantiation wasn't declared an article of faith until the Fourth Lateran Council in 1215. With Luther, we confess:

> Concerning transubstantiation, we do by no means regard the subtle sophistry, in which they teach that bread and wine part with, or lose their natural essence, the form and color only remaining, but are no longer real bread and wine ; for it corresponds best with the Scripture, that bread is and remains here, as St. Paul himself calls it "The bread which we break," 1 Cor. 10:16. "And so let him eat of that bread," 1 Cor. 11:28.

---

[16] Book IV.18.5 in vol. 1, p. 486, in *The Ante-Nicene Fathers*, ed. Alexander Roberts and James Donaldson, 10 vols. (1885–1887; repr., Peabody, MA: Hendrickson, 1994), hereafter ANF.

[17] ANF I:185 n.6

Consubstantiation

Q: I had always understood that Lutherans believed in Consubstantiation, but you clarified that Lutheran belief should be understood as sacramental union, meaning that Our Lord's Body and Blood are united with the bread and wine. Further, I believe Sacramental Union means that Our Lord's Body and Blood are "in, with, and under" the bread and wine. Am I correct to understand that the bread and wine are vehicles for the Body and Blood of Our Lord but are not completely changed into the Body and Blood of Our Lord? Then, at the end of Communion, there remains some of the Body and Blood of Our Lord, are they consumed, or do you keep some (i.e. the Body) reserved for the home bound and the sick? Would you kindly explain how consubstantiation differs from Sacramental Union?

A: Nearly everybody believes that Lutherans believe in consubstantiation. It's commonly held to mean that both bread and wine and Christ's true body and blood are simultaneously present in the Lord's Supper. That's what Lutherans believe. But that's not consubstantiation. What's consubstantiation? The Christian Cyclopedia defines consubstantiation as being two possible errant beliefs about Christ's presence in the Sacrament. It defines consubstantiation as either a

> View, falsely charged to Lutheranism, that bread and body form 1 substance (a "3d substance") in Communion (similarly wine and blood) or that body and blood are present, like bread and wine, in a natural manner.[18]

The first option for consubstantiation is that the bread and Christ's body merge into one and the same substance, which is a third "thing" that is neither bread or body. I've never heard of anyone using Consubstantiation to mean this. The second

---

[18] http://cyclopedia.lcms.org/display.asp?t1=c&word=CONSUBSTANTIATION (Accessed July 9, 2020)

option is one that Lutherans are continually accused of holding by the Reformed, namely, that Christ's true body and blood are present in, with, and under the bread and in "in a natural manner." Those final words, "in a natural manner," are the key to understanding why Lutherans outright reject consubstantiation. By "natural manner" it means that Christ is present in a local, spatial way.

To understand why this is wrong we have to review Christ's three modes of presence. The first mode of presence, or way that Christ can be present, it called the comprehensible, or bodily mode. This was the way of being present Christ used when He walked upon the earth. His body occupied and vacated space. This is only mode of presence that you and I have. We can only be one place at one time and we take up a certain amount of space. We are locally present. The second mode of presence is "the incomprehensible, spiritual mode, in which he is not circumscribed in space, but penetrates through all creatures, where he pleases" (FC SD VIII.100). Christ can be bodily present in a way that doesn't occupy space. The Formula of Concord states, "This method he employed when he arose from the sealed sepulchre, and when he passed through the closed doors, and when he is in the bread and wine in the Lord's Supper, and as it is believed, when he was born of his mother." (Ibid). In this "spiritual" mode of presence, Christ is bodily, physically present in such a way that He doesn't take up space. The third mode of presence is that all things are present to Christ since He fills all things.

Lutherans teach that Christ is bodily present in, with, and under the bread and wine of the Lord's Supper according to the second mode of presence. He's present in a supernatural and incomprehensible way, but it's still a bodily, corporeal presence. He's just not occupying space.

The Reformed *only* believe the first mode of presence. When they hear that Christ is "in, with, and under" the bread and wine, they hear that Christ's body and blood are locally present. It must, therefore, either be enclosed within the bread and wine, which is called Impanation, or that Christ's body and blood are present in a natural way, as if my body or your body were present with bread, so that it could be seen under a microscope. The denial of other modes of presence for Christ led the Reformed to accuse Lutherans of "Capernaitic eating." In John 6:52 the unbelieving Jews ask, "How can this Man give us His flesh to eat?" Believing in only one mode of presence for Christ, the Reformed hear that we receive Christ's body and blood orally and accuse us of cannibalism. If Christ only had one mode of presence that would be the case! But Christ can be present however He wants to be. Christ is fully God. His human and divine natures are inseparable. His human nature has been glorified and receives the majesty of the divine nature. This means He can be present in the elements in a non-local way.

This kind of "local inclusion" has been rejected by Lutherans since the days of the Reformation. It was even rejected by Luther himself. He signed the Wittenberg Concord of 1536 which expressly rejected any "local inclusion" of Christ's body. Lutherans since then have adamantly rejected the term consubstantiation. It confuses the modes of Christ's presence and makes us cannibals.

So how is this different from what Lutherans believe, teach, and confess? Lutherans believe in what is called the sacramental union. Christ's very body, born of the Virgin Mary, crucified, suffered, buried, resurrected and ascended, is essentially (substantially) present in Supper, though in a way that is invisible and incomprehensible. We call this a sacramental union. It's not a natural union, nor is it a mixture of the two into one, nor is it that both "things" are taking up space in the bread and wine so that Christ's body and blood can be empirically verified. We receive the bread and wine in the natural way, that is, orally. We receive Christ's true body and blood orally as well, but in an incomprehensible and invisible way.

Consubstantiation attempts to answer the same question as Transubstantiation, "In what way is Christ truly present in the Sacrament?" or "How is Christ present in the Sacrament?" Transubstantiation goes too far by viewing the Sacrament through the lens of Aristotle. Consubstantiation either mingles or confuses the earthly and heavenly elements into one, or it assumes that Christ is present in the Supper just as He was present in the boat with the disciples. Both go beyond the Scripture to explain a mystery that Christ does not explain when He says, "Take, eat, this is my body; Drink ye all of it; For this is my blood of the new testament" (Matthew 26:26-28). Lutherans simply take Christ at His Word. The bread is simultaneously His very body offered on the cross for us. The wine is simultaneously His true blood, shed on the cross for us. He unites His body with the bread in a sacramental, incomprehensible way, and does the same with His blood and the wine, simply by the power of His Word. Both the earthly and heavenly substances are simultaneously present, but not in a consubstantiation, impanation, or anything that would imply a local presence of Christ's body and blood.

Concerning the elements that remain after everyone has communed—called Reliqua—the best practice is to consume them so that we are faithful to Christ's command to eat and drink. The reservation of the elements lead to needless questions and impious practices. Elements can be consecrated at the home or hospital bed of the sick. When the pastor is with such members, that is the manifestation of the parish in that place, so there's no need to reserve elements.

Christology and the Lord's Supper

Q: Can you explain what the Real Presence of Christ in the Eucharist has to do with Lutheran Christology—i.e., the communication of attributes? How can things that only belong to the divine nature, such as ubiquity, be communicated to the human nature? What are some examples of this, in Scripture? How does this uphold the unity of the two natures in the one person, rather than confusing them? How does this not violate the Chalcedonian definition which seems to indicate that attributes expressly do not transfer between Christ's human nature and his divine nature? How is Lutheran Christology, in this way, different from Reformed Christology?

A: Lutherans teach that Christ is one person who consists of two natures, human and divine. The two natures are united in such a close fellowship and union that they communicate, or share, attributes. Scripture describes three kinds of sharings, which Lutherans called the three genera of the communication of attributes.

The first kind of sharing we call the *genus idiomaticum*, the communication of attributes. In this genus both natures share their properties with the person of Christ, so that Christ has both human and divine attributes. Divine attributes are things like to be almighty, eternal, infinite, omnipresent, and omniscient. Human attributes are things like being flesh and blood, being circumscribed to one place at a time, being able to suffer and die. The Word possesses both sets of attributes because of the personal union, but the two natures don't comingle or mix so that the properties of one nature become the essential properties of the other nature. This genera merely teaches that the Word made flesh, Christ, has both divine and human attributes. So the rulers of this age "crucified the Lord of glory," (1 Cor. 2:8). The Son of God "was born of the seed of

David according to the flesh" (Romans 1:3). This why we say things like "God died" on Good Friday, and "Mary is the Mother of God." Because of the communication of attributes, the Word possesses its own divine properties as well as human attributes.

The second kind of sharing of attributes is the *genus apotelesmaticum*. An apotelesma is a work. This means that Christ uses both natures in His works. The flesh of Christ is more than just a conduit for the divine nature. Rather, both natures can be identified in His works. He heals, which is an act of the divine nature, but He uses human words, or touch, or spit. He says in John 6:51, "The bread that I shall give is My flesh, which I shall give for the life of the world." His human flesh gives life, an act of the divine nature.

The third kind of sharing of attributes is the *genus majestaticum*, the communication of majesty. This means that the divine nature shares its divine power and majesty with the human nature of Christ, so that the human nature is capable of things beyond its natural properties. The *Formula of Concord* says: "For to quicken, to have all judgment and all power in heaven and on earth, to have all things in His hands, to have all things in subjection beneath His feet, to cleanse from sin, etc., are not created gifts, but divine, infinite properties; and yet, according to the declaration of Scripture, these have been given and communicated to the man Christ, John 5:27; 6:39; Matt. 28:18; Dan. 7:14; John 3:35; 13:3; Matt. 11:27; Eph. 1:22; Heb. 2:8; 1 Cor. 15:27; John 1:3." This genera is the important one for Christ being present in the Lord's Supper. Because the divine nature shares its power and majesty with Christ's human nature, Christ's flesh can be present where Christ promises and it gives life and forgives sins.

This divine presence isn't ubiquitous. During the latter part of the Lutheran Reformation, the Sacramentarians—so called because they denied Christ's real presence in the Sacrament of the Altar—accused the Lutherans of teaching a general ubiquity of Christ's body, because where Christ is, He'll be there according to both natures. Lutherans have never taught a general ubiquity of Christ's human nature. The *Formula of Concord* denies that "the human nature in Christ is everywhere present in the same mode as the divinity, as an infinite essence, by essential power and property of its nature." We also deny that "the humanity of Christ is locally extended in all places of heaven and earth; which is to be ascribed not even to the divinity" (FC SD VIII.90, 92). Ubiquity, as the Sacramentarians meant it, means that Christ's body is everywhere, in every tree, rock, tankard of beer, and piece of moldy cheese (those are actually their examples). Lutherans confess that is not how the divine presence works. God isn't "locally extended" in all places in heaven and earth. Rather, God is present to all things and all things are present to Him. Since the divine nature communicates its attributes with His human nature, Christ's human nature isn't present as an infinite essence, in some pantheistic sense, but that Christ "fills all in all" as St. Paul says in Ephesians 1:22.

This means Christ can be bodily present wherever He's promised to be. Where has He promised to be present? He promises in Matthew 18:20, "For where two or three are gathered together in My name, I am there in the midst of them." He promises in Matthew 28:20, "Lo, I am with you always, even to the end of the age." Since Christ's two natures are inseparably united in the incarnation and will be inseparably united into eternity, when Christ promises to be present He is present according to both natures, human and divine. There's only one Christ. You can't separate His human nature from the divine. Now does this mean that when the Church gathers Christ is present? Yes. Does it mean we'll see

Him? No, because Christ has more than one "mode of presence" by which He can be present, meaning that Christ can be physically present in such a way that He doesn't yield physical space.

Since the Sacramentarians don't believe in the communication of attributes, they believe that the human nature of Christ doesn't receive anything from the divine nature but only acts as a conduit for the divine nature's power. Sacramentarians assume that Jesus' human body has to behave by the rules of our human bodies. Since we can only be in one place at a time, so Christ's body can only be in one place at a time. The Reformed lock Jesus' body away in heaven, as it were, imagining the right hand of God is a spatial, circumscribed place, rather than what Scripture says it is: the power of God (Exodus 15:16; Luke 22:69). Because the right hand of God isn't a physical place, but is everywhere, this means Christ can be physically present wherever He's promised to be. This includes the Lord's Supper since He promises that the bread is His body and the wine is His true blood.

The Council of Chalcedon in AD 451 stated the Christ

> must be confessed to be in two natures, unconfusedly, immutably, indivisibly, inseparably [united], and that without the distinction of natures being taken away by such union, but rather the peculiar property of each nature being preserved and being united in one Person and subsistence, not separated or divided into two persons, but one and the same Son and only-begotten, God the Word, our Lord Jesus Christ.[19]

---

[19] *The Definition of Faith of the Council of Chalcedon*in in vol. 14, p. 264-265 in *The Nicene and Post Nicene Fathers*. Second Series. Edited by Philip Schaff and Henry Wace. 14 vols. 1890–1900. Reprint, Peabody, MA: Hendrickson, 1994. Hereafter NPNF[2].

Lutheran theology upholds Chalcedon by acknowledging the two natures of Christ as indivisible and inseparable in the one person of Christ. We also uphold the definition by our confession that Christ's two natures aren't to be confused or commingled, so that one nature changes into the other. It's actually the Reformed who have trouble with Chalcedon because they separate the two natures, locking Christ away in a special spot in heaven while allowing Him to be present according to His divinity elsewhere. The Reformed also have trouble with the Council of Ephesus in AD 431 because it taught the communication of attributes in its statements about the flesh of Christ being truly life-giving.

The real presence of Christ in the Lord's Supper is clear from the *words of institution*. Lutheran Christology shows how that real presence is possible. Because of the personal union and the communication of attributes, Christ can be present with His body wherever He wills, and especially where He's promised in His Word. Because of the personal union and the *genus majestaticum*, Christ truly gives us His flesh to eat and His blood to drink in the Sacrament for the forgiveness of all our sins.

John 6 and Holy Communion

Q: Can John 6:51-56 be used as a proof text for the real presence of Christ in the Lord's Supper? Jesus says, "I am the living bread which came down from heaven. If anyone eats of this bread, he will live forever; and the bread that I shall give is My flesh, which I shall give for the life of the world. The Jews therefore quarreled among themselves, saying, 'How can this Man give us His flesh to eat?' Then Jesus said to them, 'Most assuredly, I say to you, unless you eat the flesh of the Son of Man and drink His blood, you have no life in you. 'Whoever eats My flesh and drinks My blood has eternal life, and I will raise him up at the last day. For My flesh is food indeed, and My blood is drink indeed. He who eats My flesh and drinks My blood abides in Me, and I in him.'"

A: While it's tempting to read Jesus' words in John 6 to be about the Lord's Supper, the oral eating of His body and blood in the Sacrament isn't what Jesus is teaches in this chapter. He teaches the spiritual eating of His flesh and drinking of His blood. The text presents us with several reasons for this. First, Jesus had not yet instituted the Sacrament of eating His body and drinking His blood under the bread and wine. John 6 takes place a year before the Passover during which Jesus instituted the Sacrament. Since He hadn't instituted the Sacrament yet, it wouldn't be appropriate to teach about it, especially to a crowd of unbelievers (John 6:36; 66).

Second, although Jesus speaks of eating His flesh and drinking His blood, He doesn't give them bread and wine to eat and drink in conjunction with His words. At the last supper He gives bread and wine and says, "take, eat," and "drink of it all of you." In John 6 there is no command to orally eat.

Third, the eating and drinking Jesus speaks of us is necessary for salvation. He says in John 6:53, "Most assuredly, I say to you, unless you eat the flesh of the Son of Man and drink His blood, you have no life in you." Those who don't eat Christ's flesh and drink His blood don't have His life within them. If He were teaching about the Lord's Supper then this would mean that partaking of the Lord's Supper is necessary for salvation. This leads to strange places like the practice of infant communion. These are the reasons we say that Christ isn't teaching about the Lord's Supper in John 6.

Jesus is teaching the metaphorical, or spiritual eating of His flesh and drinking of His blood here. Augustine of Hippo wrote in *City of God*, "In fine, He Himself, when He says, 'He that eateth my flesh and drinketh my blood, dwelleth in me, and I in him,' shows to what it is in reality, and not sacramentally, to eat His body and drink His blood; for this is to dwell in Christ, that He also may dwell in us."[20] He also says in Tractate 26 on John, "For to believe on Him is to eat the living bread. He that believes eats; he is sated invisibly, because invisibly is he born again. A babe within, a new man within. Where he is made new, there he is satisfied with food."[21] The eating Christ speaks of isn't the sacramental eating of His flesh under the bread and wine. The eating and drinking of Christ is faith in His Word.

Luther and the Reformers followed Augustine in this. Luther preached,

> This cannot be applied to the Sacrament. For many take
> the latter [the sacrament] to their damnation and
> judgment; it does not confer eternal life on them, for they

---

[20] Augustine, *City of God*, Book 21, Ch. 25, in vol. 2, p. 473 in *The Nicene and Post-Nicene Fathers*. First Series. Edited by Philip Schaff. 14 vols. 1886–1889. Reprint, Peabody, MA: Hendrickson, 1994. Hereafter NPNF[1.]

[21] Augustine, *Tractate 26 on John*, 1 (NFPF[1] 7:168)

have not been taught and drawn by the Father. Christ is speaking here of the chief doctrine, of the true Christian faith, which demands no more or not less than that you believe in His flesh and blood. If you do not cleave to His flesh and blood by faith, you are lost, whether you are Turk or Jew. Christ expressed this in the article: If you wish to be a Christian, you must believe in the flesh and blood of Christ.[22]

Lutherans confess this to be a spiritual eating and drinking of faith. We confess:

Now, there are two modes of partaking of the flesh of Christ; the one is spiritual, concerning which Christ, John 6:54, especially speaks, and which is effected only by the Spirit and by faith, in the preaching and in the meditation on the Gospel, even as the same is effected in the sacrament of the Lord's Supper ; and this spiritual eating is useful and salutary in itself, and necessary to all Christians, at all times, for salvation ; without which spiritual partaking, even that sacramental or oral eating in the Lord's Supper, is not only unprofitable, but also injurious and culpable. But this spiritual eating is nothing else but faith, that is, to hear the Word of God, (in which is offered unto us Christ, true God and man,—with all the blessings which he obtained for us with his body given unto death for us, and with his blood shed for us—namely, the grace of God, remission of sins, righteousness, and eternal life,) to embrace the same with faith, to apply it to ourselves, to rely firmly and with perfect confidence and assurance upon this consolation that we have a gracious God and eternal life for the sake of the Lord Jesus Christ, and to support ourselves by it in every time of need and in all temptations. (FC SD VII:61-62)

---

[22] AE 23:118

The eating and drinking Jesus speaks of is faith in His Word. This aligns with what Jesus says in John 6 because faith is necessary for salvation. No one is justified without faith in Christ's promise. What He's telling the crowd in John 6 is, "Believe my teaching and place your confidence in my Gospel." This is similar to the way Jesus compares Himself and His Gospel to a great supper in the parable of Luke 14:16-24. In the parable the man invited people to come and enjoy the feast; that is, hear the Gospel of Christ and believe, to feast on Christ and His benefits by faith. This is the spiritual eating of Christ which "If anyone eats of this bread, he will live forever" (John 6:51), so that believers abide in Him and He in them.

There is also the oral or sacramental eating of Christ in the Sacrament. That's what Jesus bids us do in the words of institution. Even with that though, the spiritual eating and drinking of Christ is necessary. When you eat and drink Christ's body and blood sacramentally, you must also be believing His Words, "This is my body, given for you," "This is my blood, shed for you for the remission of sins." The *Formula of Concord* addresses this:

> The other mode of partaking of the body of Christ is *oral* or *sacramental*, when in the Lord's Supper, the true, essential body and blood of Christ are received and partaken of orally, by all who eat and drink the consecrated bread and wine, in this holy sacrament. Believers receive the body and blood of Christ as a sure pledge and confirmation that their sins are certainly remitted, and that Christ dwells and is efficacious in them ; unbelievers, also, receive the body and blood of Christ orally, but to their judgment and condemnation. This the words of Christ, which he used in the institution of this sacrament, expressly teach. For, at the table and during the Supper, he administered natural bread and natural

wine to his disciples, which he calls his true body and his true blood, and says at the same time : *Eat,* and *drink.* Hence this command of Christ, in consequence of the circumstances connected with it, can be understood not otherwise than as relating to an oral eating and drinking, not in a gross, carnal, Capernaitic,* but in a supernatural, incomprehensible manner. Besides this oral eating, Christ, in his other command, afterwards requires another and spiritual eating, when he further says : "This do in remembrance of me ;" for here he demands faith. (FC SD VII: 63-65)

While Jesus isn't speaking of the Lord's Supper in John 6, but the spiritual eating of His flesh and blood, there is a connection between this and the sacramental eating of Christ. In order to enjoy the benefits of the sacramental eating and drinking of Christ's flesh and blood, the communicant must also spiritually partake of Christ by faith. If someone eats Christ's flesh sacramentally without eating Christ spiritually by faith, he "eats and drinks judgment to himself" (1 Corinthians 11:29). Martin Chemnitz explains the compatibility between the spiritual and sacramental eating and drinking in this way:

Thus in order that the eating which was instituted in the Lord's Supper might not take place unto judgment but rather unto salvation, it is necessary to add the spiritual eating which is described in John 6. So we receive and embrace the body of Christ, which we receive orally in the Lord's Supper, with the same faith with which, outside the use of the Supper, Christ wills that His flesh be eaten (John 6) . . . that is, the spiritual eating of John 6 is confirmed and sealed by this eating which was instituted in the Supper.[23]

---

[23] Martin Chemnitz, The Lord's Supper, trans. J.A.O. Preus (St. Louis, MO: Concordia Publishing House, 1979), 239.

While John 6 is related to the Lord's Supper, it doesn't prove Christ's bodily presence in, with, and under the bread and wine in the Lord's Supper. There is no need for other texts to prove Christ's real presence in the Sacrament, since He Himself plainly says, "This is My body. This is My blood." The worthy communicant takes Christ at His wordm that the bread is His very body and the wine is His very blood, given to us to eat and drink for our forgiveness, salvation, and newness of life.

Drinking Jesus Blood and Docetism

Q: I was interacting with a fellow online who appears to hold to a symbolic understanding (or at the very least, a spiritual understanding) of the Sacraments, and he brought up the fact that Jesus Christ was not crucified prior to His administration of the Supper to the apostles. He stated that, as being under the Old Covenant, Jesus would have been breaking the Law by telling the apostles to eat His flesh and drink His blood. He also implied that holding to a Real Presence view takes one into Docetism (not sure how that works, since Docetism denies an actual fleshly presence of Jesus). How does Lutheranism speak to the Real Presence with regard to Maundy Thursday and the Supper given that night?

A: On the night in which Jesus was betrayed He took bread and said, "Take, eat; this is My body" (Matthew 26:26). He then took the cup and said, "Drink from it, all of you. For this is My blood of the new covenant, which is shed for many for the remission of sins" (Matthew 26:27-28).

In Genesis 9:3-4 the Lord gave every moving thing that lives" as food for mankind. However, the Lord told Noah, "You shall not eat flesh with its life, that is, its blood." He further establishes this in the Mosaic Law, several times legislating that Israel wasn't to eat the blood of animals. Leviticus 19:26 states, "You shall not eat anything with the blood." The reason is the same as it was in Noah's day. The life of the flesh is the blood. This is why the blood of Israel's sacrifices was to make atonement for them (Lev. 17:11) and never to be imbibed. Since Christ "knew no sin" (2 Corinthians 5:21) and "was in all points tempted as we are, yet without sin" (Hebrews 4:15), He would not have commanded His apostles to violate the very law He came to fulfill in our place. Does this mean that Christ spoke figuratively of eating His body and drinking His blood?

If Jesus gave His flesh to eat and His blood to drink in a natural way, then He would be commanding cannibalism and drinking of blood contrary to the Law of Moses. Lutherans confess in the *Formula of Concord* that this eating is "not in a gross, carnal, Capernaitic, but in a supernatural, incomprehensible manner" (FC SD VII.64).

The *Apology of the Book of Concord* explains,

> Now because this eating and drinking does not occur in a natural way, the way one eats other flesh, it must occur in a different, supernatural, heavenly way, which Christ has reserved for it. . . His body and blood are truly present with the bread and wine, but not in such a way that His body and blood in themselves are crushed with the teeth, masticated, and swallowed. Rather, they are present by virtue of the sacramental union, as when Scripture says that the Holy Spirit was seen and descended like a dove [cf. Matt. 3:16].[24]

Christ's true body and blood are present in, with, and under the bread and wine in an incomprehensible way, not a natural way as if your flesh or blood was present in bread and wine. Because of the sacramental union of the earthly and heavenly elements, Christ's very body, born of the Virgin Mary, crucified, suffered, buried, resurrected and ascended, is essentially (substantially) present in the Supper, though in a way that is invisible and incomprehensible. We receive the bread and wine in the natural way, that is, orally. We receive Christ's true body and blood orally as well, but in an incomprehensible and invisible way. Christ's body and blood are truly present and we receive them orally, but not in a natural way.

---

[24] Martin Chemnitz, Timothy Kirchner, and Nicolaus Selnecker. *Apology or Vindication of the Christian Book of Concord,* ed. Kevin Walker, trans. James Langebartels (St. Louis, MO: Concordia Publishing House, 2018), 290-291.

This is also how Jesus gave His disciples His true body and blood to eat and drink on the night in which He was betrayed. Being the eternal Son of God, fully divine, He has more than one way of being present. Sitting at the table with the disciples He is locally present, as you and I are locally present in one place. But according to His Word, His body and blood are present in the bread and wine in an invisible, incomprehensible way.[25]

The second accusation, that holding to Christ's real presence in the Sacrament takes one into Docetism, is absurd. Docetism is the belief that Jesus didn't really have a body, but only seemed to have a body. The name comes from the Greek word dokeo (δοκέω) which means "to think, seem, or suppose." So Jesus only seemed to have a body. He was a phantom. This belief arose in the second half of the first century A.D.. St. John addresses Docetism in his first epistle. He begins in 1:1 by writing about the reality of Jesus' body, "That which was from the beginning, which we have heard, which we have seen with our eyes, which we have looked upon, and our hands have handled." He writes in 2 John 1:7, "For many deceivers have gone out into the world who do not confess Jesus Christ as coming in the flesh."

By teaching Jesus was only a phantasm or hologram, Docetism denies the chief doctrine of the Christian faith, the incarnation of God the Son, that the second person of the Holy Trinity assumed human flesh to redeem us from sin and death. If God the Son did not assume our flesh, then our flesh isn't redeemed.

Ignatius of Antioch (died ca. 107), writing at the very beginning of the second century, addressed Docetism in several of his epistles. He writes in Ephesians 7:2, "There is only one physician, who is both flesh and spirit, born and unborn, God in man, true life in death, both from Mary and from God, first

---

[25] See the chapter entitled *Christology and the Lord's Supper*.

subject to suffering and then beyond it, Jesus Christ our Lord." He writes in Smyrnaeans 1:2 that Christ was "truly nailed in the flesh for us under Pontius Pilate and Herod the tetrarch." His fullest confession that Christ had a true, physical body comes in Smyrnaeans 3:1-2,

> For I know and believe that he was in the flesh even after the resurrection; and when he came to Peter and those with him, he said to them: 'Take hold of me; handle me and see that I am not a disembodied demon.' And immediately they touched him and believed, being closely united with his flesh and blood. For this reason they too despised death; indeed, they proved to be greater than death. And after his resurrection he ate and drank with them like one who is composed of flesh, although spiritually he was united with the Father.

Christ's resurrection in the flesh—what else can resurrection mean?—gave the apostles reason to think little of death for the sake of Christ.

In Ignatius' confession of Christ's true flesh against the Docetists He teaches how the incarnation of God the Son means that Christ's true flesh and blood is present in the Lord's Supper. He writes in Romans 7:3, "I take no pleasure in corruptible food or the pleasures of this life. I want the bread of God, which is the flesh of Christ who is of the seed of David; and for drink I want his blood, which is incorruptible love." Because Christ has true flesh and blood, that's what He gives us in the Eucharist.

Ignatius even tells us that the Docetists refrain from the Eucharist precisely *because* they deny it is Christ's true body and blood. He writes in Smyrnaeans 6:2, "They abstain from Eucharist and prayer because they refuse to acknowledge that the Eucharist is the flesh of our savior Jesus Christ, which suffered for our sins and which the Father by his goodness raised up." Since the Docetists refused to believe that Jesus had a true human body they had no reason to participate in the Eucharist since the church taught that it was the very flesh and blood of Christ.

The accusation that belief in Christ's real presence in the Sacrament leads to the heresy of Docetism is backwards. Those who deny the bodily presence of Christ in the Lord's Supper have more in common with the ancient Docetists than those who affirm His bodily presence in the Eucharist.

Repentance and Communion

Q: The pastor in my congregation denied a homosexual man the Lord's Supper. He lives with another man. While some argue that as an openly gay man he doesn't show regret for his sin, others say that the Sacrament which renews and strengthens faith could be the help he needs to change his life. As a fellow minister what would be your attitude towards the situation and how does the scripture support that?

A: Your pastor made the right call for two reasons. First, the man is involved in public sin and shows no sign of penitence. Second, the Sacrament is intended for the penitent who are sorry for their sin, desire forgiveness, and intend to amend their life.

Let's break this down. The man is involved in a public homosexual relationship. It's public because he's openly gay and living with another man. To choose to cohabit outside of marriage is intentional sin, whether the couple is heterosexual or homosexual. As a cohabiting heterosexual couple shouldn't be communed because they are living in impenitence, neither should a homosexual cohabiting couple be communed. Both are living in impenitent, public sin. The fact that he's an openly homosexual man, meaning that he sees no problem with his behavior, also shows his impenitence.

The suggestion that he should be allowed the Sacrament because it strengthens faith and could be the help he needs to change his life confuses the law and the gospel and makes the Sacrament into something it's not. The Sacrament was instituted to give the forgiveness of sins to sinners who, upon examining themselves, recognize their sins, sorrow over them, and intend to amend their ways. Amendment means to abstain from those sins and to pursue the opposite virtue. When a person takes the Lord's Supper without repentance and faith in

Christ's promise to forgive sins, he communes unworthily. The Formula of Concord teaches:

> For, the fact that not only godly, pious, and believing Christians, but unworthy and ungodly hypocrites — persons, for instance, like Judas and his associates, who have no spiritual communion with Christ, and approach the table of the Lord, without true repentance and conversion to God—also receive the true body and blood of Christ in the Sacrament orally, and by their unworthy eating and drinking commit a grievous sin against the body and blood of Christ—this fact St. Paul expressly teaches. (FC SD VII.60)

To commune without repentance is to grievously sin against Christ's body and blood. The Lord's Supper wasn't instituted to bring men to repentance. God gave His law to bring men to repentance. The Lord's Supper was instituted to forgive the sins of those whom the law has already brought to repentance. In this situation, the law needs to be brought to bear on this man so that he recognizes the severity of his sin and God's wrath against the impenitent. Only when he truly repents, confesses his sin and receives absolution, and bears the fruit of repentance, which in this case means ending the relationship, moving out, and intending to be abstinent and chaste, can he be admitted to the Lord's Table, which will again offer him the forgiveness of his sins and strengthen his faith.

Judas was mentioned a moment ago in the quotation from the *Formula of Concord*. It's true that Judas was present when Christ instituted the Sacrament and partook of it. By that point he had already decided to betray Jesus. He had already received the thirty pieces of silver and was seeking an opportunity to betray Jesus. Yet, Jesus allows him to celebrate the supper.

This shouldn't be read as an open invitation to impenitent sinners to come to the Lord's Table. Jesus says in Luke 22:21-22, "But behold, the hand of My betrayer is with Me on the table. And truly the Son of Man goes as it has been determined, but woe to that man by whom He is betrayed!" The other disciples "began to question among themselves, which of them it was who would do this thing" (Luke 22:23). These verses show us two things. First, Judas' sin wasn't publicly known to the disciples at this time. Only Jesus knew of Judas' sin. Second, Jesus takes one final opportunity to admonish Judas to repent and put his sin away. It wasn't receiving the Lord's Supper that could have brought Judas to repentance. It was Jesus' word of law pronouncing woe on him as long as he remained in his sin. Johann Gerhard noted this and wrote:

> Accordingly, a distinction is to be made among sinners. Those who fall into sin unknowingly or in weakness and are overtaken with by failure (Gal. 6:1)—but who confess their sin, trust in the Lord Christ, and promise to amend their ways–such sinners one should not exclude from the holy supper, for Christ instituted it for the sake of tormented anxious sinners. Also, if the sin is secret, that is, known only to the preacher or indeed only to a few others, thus in the same way one should not exclude the sinner, but faithfully admonish him and allow him, on his conscience, to attend the Supper. However, if the sinner lies in public and known sin, promises no amendment, and by deed indicates none, one should by no means admit him to the holy supper.[26]

The Lord's Supper is for those who confess their sin, trust in the Lord Christ, and promise to amend their ways. Christ has instituted the Sacrament for sinners who feel their sins and want to be rid of them. Nor should sinners be excluded if the

---

[26] Gerhard, *Comprehensive Explanation*, 424-425.

pastor and a few others know about it, again, assuming there is repentance, the desire for forgiveness, and the honest intention to amend the sinful life. As Martin Chemnitz says, "For this medicine has been prepared and provided for the sick who acknowledge their infirmity and seek counsel and help."[27]

The Lord's Supper is not for those who refuse to acknowledge their sin and confess it. The *Formula of Concord* teaches that this is what makes one an unworthy communicant. It reads:

> But it should be carefully explained who the unworthy guests of this holy Supper are ; they are those who approach this sacrament, without true repentance and sorrow for their sins, without true faith, and without a good intention to amend their lives, and who by their unworthy oral eating of the body of Christ, incur judgment, that is, temporal and eternal chastisements, and become guilty of the body and blood of Christ. (FC SD VII.68)

Since this gentleman is living in public sin and shows no signs of amendment, he shouldn't be admitted to the Lord's Supper. If he communed he would sin against the body and blood of Christ and drink more judgment upon himself. If the pastor was to commune him, this would only show the man that his behavior isn't sin and he has no reason to repentant. That's the opposite of what he needs to hear right now. May the Lord bring him to repentance and faith in Christ, who has earned forgiveness for every sin and wants to forgive the penitent who flees to Him.

---

[27] Martin Chemnitz, *Ministry, Word, and Sacraments, An Enchiridion*, trans. Luther Poell0t, (St. Louis, MO: Concordia Publishing House, 1981), 132.

Which Churches Have the Lord's Supper?

Q: Who in this list is receiving the true body and blood of Christ in Communion? Baptists teach the bread and grape juice are symbols of Christ's presence. Roman Catholicism teaches transubstantiation. Eastern Orthodoxy teaches the Lord's Supper as a divine mystery. Calvinists hold to a spiritual presence of Christ in the Lord's Supper, while some Anglicans believe in Christ's real presence, but I know not all do though. Which one of these is truly receiving the true body and blood of Christ objectively in the bread and wine? Put crudely - is Jesus present in all these communions, or only in some? If so, which ones is he present in, and why? Is it based on the believer's faith that makes him present, or the profession of the church community?

A: Churches which use the words of institution properly have the Sacrament, both in essence and in effect. The essence of the Lord's Supper is the material, that is, the true body and blood of Christ under the bread and wine. The effect of the Sacrament is the forgiveness of sins. In those churches were the Words of Christ are falsified and publicly confessed to mean the opposite of what they plainly say, there is no Sacrament in essence or effect. Christ's body and blood aren't present nor is the forgiveness of sins given through that celebration.

Consider how this works in Holy Baptism. There are churches which deny the effect of Baptism. For instance, Baptists deny that the Triune God regenerates sinners and forgives sins through the waters of Holy Baptism. The Roman Catholic Church impairs the effects of Baptism by teaching that it only forgives sins committed prior to baptism, so that penance and purgatory are necessary to cleanse one from sins committed after baptism. Both the Papist and the Baptist deny, to one extend or another, the effects of Baptism. But BOTH groups use the baptismal formula and publically confess the Triune God in whose name we are commanded to baptize. So the baptism of the Baptists and Papists is valid because they confess the Triune God in whose name the baptism is done, even though they deny and impair the effect.

But now consider the Jehovah's Witness. They use the baptismal formula but the public confession of the Jehovah's Witness is Unitarian not Trinitarian. So even when they use the words of the baptismal formula, by their denial of the Trinity they have twisted and abolished the very words they use. Thus they don't have a Christian baptism because they deny the essence of Baptism, that is, that it is the baptism of the Triune God, Father, Son, and Holy Ghost. This is why, when a former Jehovah's Witness joins a Christian church, he's baptized because his baptism from the Jehovah's Witnesses was not a Christian baptism in the first place.

So which churches have Christ bodily present to forgive sins in the Sacrament? The Papist church publicly confesses the real presence of Christ. Therefore, they have the Sacrament; although, it's important to note that Rome mutilates the Sacrament through its doctrine of Transubstantiation and the fact that many dioceses still only distribute the Lord's body to the communicant, not the blood. But Rome confesses Christ's bodily presence. The same goes for the Eastern Church, with similar, though not identical reservations.

Once you get into Reformed Protestantism things change though. Baptists, Methodists, Church of Christ, Assembly of God, Bible churches, and the like, publicly confess that Christ is not truly and bodily present in the Lord's Supper. Their public confession is that the words of Jesus don't mean what they say. Whether they teach that the bread and wine are symbols of Christ's absent body, or that the bread and wine are a communion with the spirit of Christ in heaven, or any of the other various Reformed explanations of the Lord's Supper is irrelevant. If the congregation's public confession is that Christ's Words mean something other than what they plainly say, that congregation twists and abolishes Christ's word so that when they celebrate the Lord's Supper, it is not the Sacrament in essence or effect. Christ is not bodily present under the bread and wine. Nor are sins forgiven in that celebration. As for Anglicans, the *Thirty-Nine Articles* present a Calvinian understanding of the Lord's Supper, but like you, I've met several Anglicans that believe in the bodily presence of Christ in the Sacrament. The best I can say in that situation is that it's doubtful that Christ is bodily present. If an Anglican truly believes in Christ's real presence, he should leave that fellowship for one that confesses what the Scriptures teach.

The bottom line is that the Word makes Christ present in the Supper. So in churches that don't teach that Christ's Word is true, there is no Sacrament there. If Christ is bodily present then they would be drinking judgment on themselves each time they have the Supper, according to 1 Corinthians 11:29. Thank God that's not happening. But since their preachers are falsifying Christ's words in the name of the Lord, their teachers sin against the second commandment by teaching falsehood in God's name.

Since its Christ's Word which effects the Sacrament this also means that the faith of each individual communicant does not effect the Sacrament. The teaching that the bread and wine don't become Christ's body and blood until they're received by the believing communicant is called Receptionism. Receptionism takes the efficacy of the Sacrament away from the Words of Christ and locates it in the faith of communicant. St. Augustine specifically condemns Receptionism when he writes against the Donatists:

When one asks about the completeness or holiness of the whole sacrament, nothing depends on the faith or the kind of faith or the one who receives the sacrament. Much depends on this faith as far as the blessedness or blessed use of the sacrament is concerned; but nothing depends on this faith as far the question of the sacrament itself is concerned. For it can easily happen that someone has the entire sacrament and yet has a wrong faith.[28]

The words of Christ, properly confessed by the congregation and used by the pastor, effects the Sacrament so that Christ is bodily present in, with, and under the bread and wine. Faith in Christ's words, which discern that Christ is bodily present, receives Christ's body and blood for blessing and benefit. If the communicant does not believe Christ's Words, he still receives Christ's body and blood, not for forgiveness of sins but judgment unless he repents and believes.

---

[28] Augustine, *On Baptism*, translation from *The Apology of the Book of Concord*, 241.

Communion in Areas without Bread

Q: If the Bread and Wine are means of Grace, what about people, past and present, that have lived in regions where wheat and grapes aren't produced. Why would God deny them this means of Grace, such as in Asia rice was grown throughout history not wheat? Could rice flour be used for the bread?

A: Christ instituted the Sacrament of His Body and Blood using natural bread and natural wine. Matthew 26:26 says, "Jesus took bread." In Matthew 26:29 Jesus calls what's in the chalice the "fruit of the vine." Whenever the Lord's Supper is spoken of in Scripture it is always described as bread and the cup which contains the fruit of the vine. Natural Bread and natural wine are the essential elements that constitute the Lord's Supper.[29] But what do we mean by "natural bread?" There are, after all, all sorts of things that can be milled into flour these days, some grains, others not. There are also "fruit of the vine" besides grapes. Rice can be milled into flour to make bread. Tomatoes and blackberries can be fermented to make wine. Since bread with rice flour is still bread and tomatoes and blackberries are fruit of the vine, can these be substituted if the other elements are unavailable?

Whenever the question of substituting elements comes up, the words of the *Formula of Concord* must be remembered. "If the institution of Christ, as he ordained it, be not observed, it is no sacrament" (FC SD VII.85). Christ's institution includes the essential elements of bread and wine. What kind of bread and wine did Jesus use? Bread made from wheat or barely and wine fermented from grapes. These were used in Israel at the time and what everyone in the ancient world would think of when they heard the words "bread" and "wine." The problem with other grains and vine fruit is that they introduce doubt into the

---

[29] FC SD VII.37, 46, 63

validity of the Lord's Supper. Therefore, the best practice is to use bread and wine as Christ would have used: bread from wheat or barley and wine from grapes. Substitutions are to be avoided to prevent questions of certainty.

That being said, there isn't a problem with this in Asia, and if there is a lack of these earthly elements in one part of the world, there's a clear way to deal with that lack. A quick Google search shows that wheat has been grown in China since the Sui Dynasty (581–618 A.D.).[30] Wheat is cultivated in north China, India, and Japan. In 2017 China was the largest producer of grapes, accounting for almost 17% of global production.[31] So God isn't denying a means of grace to people in Asia due to a lack of the elements.

What about those places, wherever they may be, where wheat and grapes can't grow? Johann Gerhard, the arch-theologian of the Lutheran Church, had a simple answer: Import it. In his *Comprehensive Explanation of Holy Baptism and the Lord's Supper* from 1610, he wrote:

> Here again an apparent point of contention, that one cannot have available bread and wine in every locale. So in Norway one uses dried fish instead of bread; also, there grapes for wine cannot be readily grown because of the tremendously cold climate. Hence, it would be better that one use something else similar to bread and wine instead of completely omitting the administration of the Lord's Super. ANSWER: It would be difficult to mention any place on earth where bread and wine would be unavailable. Even though it doesn't grow in every place, yet it is imported. Therefore, one may readily obtain enough

---

[30]https://www.cambridge.org/core/journals/china-quarterly/article/wheat-in-chinapast-present-and-future/52495F75999C2E9E309E48C11A741529

[31] https://en.wikipedia.org/wiki/List_of_countries_by_grape_production

bread and wine to administer the holy Lord's Supper. And if, in case of an emergency, no one can obtain bread and wine, then it is better to omit the administration of the Lord's Supper than to go against the express institution of Christ. Just as it is not to be regarded as a Baptism when the external element of water isn't used and something else is used in its place, so also it is not a Supper of the Lord, when something else is substituted for the bread and wine.[32]

If it won't grow in a certain area, import it. If you can't import it, which is highly unlikely, then don't celebrate the Lord's Supper until you have access to the proper elements. It's far better to go without the Sacrament than to go against Christ's institution, because when Christ's institution isn't followed, there's no Lord's Supper being celebrated. Nor is it helpful to substitute elements which introduce doubt into the Sacrament. A congregation can abstain from the Supper for a time until it's able to import the elements. That will also teach everyone the seriousness with which Christians should take Christ's words.

If a person or parish has to abstain from the Lord's Supper for a time it can be helpful to remember that there is a twofold eating of Christ's flesh. One is spiritual. The other is oral/sacramental. The oral eating of Christ's flesh happens when we partake of His true body and blood in the Lord's Supper. Concerning the spiritual eating of Christ's flesh the Formula of Concord says:

> Now, there are two modes of partaking of the flesh of Christ ; the one is spiritual, concerning which Christ, John 6:54, especially speaks, and which is effected only by the Spirit and by faith, in the preaching and in the meditation on the Gospel, even as the same is effected in the

---

[32] Johann Gerhard, *Comprehensive Explanation*, 228-229.

sacrament of the Lord's Supper ; and this spiritual eating is useful and salutary in itself, and necessary to all Christians, at all times, for salvation ; without which spiritual partaking, even that sacramental or oral eating in the Lord's Supper, is not only unprofitable, but also injurious and culpable.

But this spiritual eating is nothing else but faith, that is, to hear the Word of God, (in which is offered unto us Christ,—true God and man,—with all the blessings which he obtained for us with his body given unto death for us, and with his blood shed for us—namely, the grace of God, remission of sins, righteousness, and eternal life,) to embrace the same with faith, to apply it to ourselves, to rely firmly and with perfect confidence and assurance upon this consolation that we have a gracious God and eternal life for the sake of the Lord Jesus Christ, and to support ourselves by it in every time of need and in all temptations. (FC SD VII.61-62)

If a Christian or congregation can't celebrate the Sacrament and partake of Christ's flesh orally, there is still the spiritual eating of His flesh, which is simply faith in God's Word that applies Christ's benefits to oneself and relies upon those benefits in temptations. The spiritual eating of faith happens simultaneously as the oral eating of Christ's flesh in the Sacrament, but it also happens apart from the Sacrament whenever we hear the Word, believe it, and apply it to ourselves in a lively faith and confidence. This spiritual eating of Christ's flesh is what Christ has commanded faithful Christians and congregations to do whether or not they are able to partake of the Sacrament. When it comes to the Sacrament we need to stick with Christ's institution and stay away from anything that introduces questions as to whether or not it is really the Sacrament.

Why Closed Communion?

Q: Dear Pastor, why don't you allow Christians in denominations other than your own to participate in Holy Communion?

A: Historically the church has practiced what is called 'Closed Communion.' This means ministers only admit Christians with whom they are in fellowship—formal doctrinal agreement—to the Lord's Supper. The opposite practice—'Open Communion'—occurs when ministers admit those with whom they are not in fellowship to partake of the Lord's Supper. There are two reasons for practicing Closed Communion. First, when you participate in the Lord's Supper you receive Christ's true body and true blood. Second, when you commune with other Christians at a particular altar you confess that you hold the same beliefs as everyone else at that altar. Participating in the Lord's Supper is therefore communion with our Lord Jesus Christ and one another.

How is the Lord's Supper a communion with Christ? Jesus gives us His very body to eat and His very blood to drink. Jesus says: "Now as they were eating, Jesus took bread, and after blessing it he broke it and gave it to the disciples and said, 'Take, eat; this is my body.' And he took the cup, and when he had given thanks he gave it to them, saying, 'Drink of it, all of you, for this is my blood of the covenant, which is poured out for many for the forgiveness of sins'" (Matthew 26:26-28; also in Mark 14:22-24; Luke 22:19-20; and 1 Corinthians 11:23-25).

Christ's Word is spoken over the bread and wine by His called servant of the Word, the pastor. After this consecration, the pastor distributes Christ's body and blood to those under his pastoral care. Dr. Luther teaches in the *Small Catechism* that a person is truly worthy and well-prepared who has faith in these words: "Given and shed for you for the forgiveness of sins." This requires that the communicant be instructed in Christian doctrine so that he is contrite for his sins and seeks the blessings Christ offers in the Sacrament. It also requires that he be able to "discern the body" of Christ in the Sacrament.

If someone doesn't believe Jesus' words, then the Lord's real body and blood in the Sacrament does not bring blessings, but judgment. Paul writes to the Corinthians, "For anyone who eats and drinks without recognizing the body of the Lord eats and drinks judgment on himself. That is why many among you are weak and sick and a number of you have fallen asleep" (1 Corinthians 11:29-30). The pastor is also held responsible before God's judgment if he does not take great care to administer the Lord's Supper faithfully and not to anyone's detriment (Ezekiel 33:8-9). The pastor is Christ's steward (1 Corinthians 4:1) and must administer Christ's blessings to those who are penitent and believing.

The Lord's Supper is also a communion with one another. Unlike Baptism, the Lord's Supper is a Sacrament that occurs not one-by-one, but with the whole congregation at once. It shows complete unity in every way with Christ and with each other. Communing at a particular altar is a public confession, or agreement, to the faith that is taught at that particular altar. Paul writes of this in 1 Corinthians 10:16-18:

> The cup of blessing that we bless, is it not a participation in the blood of Christ? The bread that we break, is it not a participation in the body of Christ? Because there is one bread, we who are many are one body, for we all partake of the one bread. Consider the people of Israel: are not those who eat the sacrifices participants in the altar?

When you participate at the altar of a particular congregation you are publicly proclaiming that you believe and confess the doctrine taught there at that altar. This confession is not limited only to an understanding of Christ's real presence in the Supper. Participation means you believe and confess as is believed and confessed in all articles of the Gospel, not just in a few of them. Participating in the Lord's Supper is a public confession of faith that the communicants are united in Christ Jesus by the same doctrine. Scripture teaches that communicants are to be united in doctrine when it says in Acts 2:42, "They continued steadfastly in the apostles' doctrine and fellowship, in the breaking of bread, and in prayers." Continuing in the apostles' doctrine leads to common participation in the breaking of bread (the Sacrament) and the prayers (worship).

Paul urges unity of belief when he tells the Corinthians, "I appeal to you, brothers, by the name of our Lord Jesus Christ, that all of you agree and that there be no divisions among you, but that you be united in the same mind and the same judgment" (1 Corinthians 1:10). Closed Communion protects the unbelieving from drinking judgment on themselves. It also protects the unity of the church's doctrine.

When members of other denominations aren't allowed to commune at an altar, that is not a judgment of their faith in Christ. It is simply taking them at their word and heeding their public confession of faith. The reason denominations exist is because there are different confessions of the Christian Faith. A person who belongs to a church or church body of a confession different from ours publicly states thereby that he or she agrees with the confession of that church and disagrees with ours. For example, if you belong to the United Methodist Church it is because you believe that the doctrine of the United Methodist Church is the apostles' doctrine. Since we believe differently than the United Methodist Church on many articles of the Christian Faith, we are not in communion with that group. The same is true even for various Lutheran church bodies with whom our congregation is not in fellowship, that is, doctrinal agreement. If there is not agreement in the apostles' doctrine, there is no communion.

When a person is denied communion at Holy Cross I'm not judging their faith or saying they aren't a Christian. I'm saying one of the two following things, either: a) that person belongs to an altar of a church that believes, teaches, and confesses contrary to the faith that is believed, taught, and confessed at our altar, or b) that person hasn't been instructed in the Biblical doctrine to express agreement. This is why the answer to "Can I commune at Holy Cross?" isn't "No." It's "not yet." Once a person is instructed in the Christian Faith as it is taught at this altar and confesses that it is their confession of the Christian Faith as well, then I gladly welcome them to Christ's altar to receive the blessings Christ gives to all worthy communicants.

The current theological climate in which we live stresses common beliefs and minimizes (or ignores) doctrinal differences. This makes the practice of Closed Communion all the more important. It protects the unbelieving from drinking judgment upon themselves and teaches the importance of doctrinal unity. Christ commands His church to confess the faith that was once delivered to the saints (Jude 3). We are to observe all things Christ commanded (Matthew 28:20), not only the ones everyone can agree upon. With this in mind, we take our confession of faith very seriously, watching our doctrine and life closely (1 Timothy 4:16). Closed Communion takes Christ's commands for doctrinal agreement and unity seriously (2 Thessalonians 3:14-15; Romans 16:17), while protecting those who have not yet been instructed in common Christian Faith of Holy Scripture. Thus Closed Communion is a practice of Christian love: Love for Christ and His word as well as love for our neighbor.

Closed Communion in the Lutheran Confessions and Church History

Q:. I'm having a debate with my pastor about how loose he does communion. He calls it closed but they only require people to be believers and be seeking forgiveness. I have been trying to impress upon him the importance of the communicants believing in the true presence by using the 1 Corinthians 11:29. I was also hoping to use the Lutheran Confessions. I looked last night but couldn't really pinpoint anything. Could you direct me to where the practice of closed communion is talked about in the confession? I thought you mentioned that it was in there in one of your videos.

A: If your pastor doesn't require communicants at his altar to believe Christ is truly present in the Sacrament, then I have to wonder if he even believes it. I don't say that to be mean. I say that because the real bodily presence of Christ in the Sacrament is the primary scriptural reason for closed communion. St. Paul writes in 1 Corinthians 11:27, "Whoever eats this bread or drinks this cup of the Lord in an unworthy manner will be guilty of the body and blood of the Lord." Eating and drinking unworthily doesn't make you guilty of a symbol of Christ's body and blood. Nor does it make you guilty of a far distant, spiritual body and blood (as if there could be such a thing). Eating and drinking unworthily makes one guilty of "the body and blood of the Lord." He writes in verses 29 "He who eats and drinks in an unworthy manner eats and drinks judgment to himself, not discerning the Lord's body." The Lord's body which is being discerned here isn't the church as the body of Christ, but it is the body and blood of Christ present in, with, and under the bread and wine. If Christ's true body and blood are present, and the pastor allows any penitent Christian to commune, regardless of their belief about Christ's body and blood, the pastor is allowing them to eat and drink judgment upon themselves, inviting them to be guilty of the body and blood of Christ. That's not loving. Nor is it pastoral. It's actually allowing people to heap judgment upon themselves. From this I can only surmise that either the pastor himself doesn't believe Christ is truly present or that he doesn't take the Office of Ministry as seriously as he ought.

As for the practice of closed communion in the Lutheran Confessions, there are two places that allude to the practice. The first is in Article 24 of the Augsburg Confession, paragraphs 34-36. Melanchthon argues against private masses and states that the Lutherans hold one communion every holy day and on other appropriate days. He then writes, "And this custom is not new in the Church; for the Fathers before Gregory make no mention of any private Mass, but of the common Mass [the Communion] they speak very much. Chrysostom says that the priest stands daily at the altar, inviting some to the Communion and keeping back others." Melanchthon uses the example of John Chrysostom (ca. 350-407) to demonstrate his point that even daily Masses were public masses, not private masses. For our purposes though, the important phrase is "inviting some to the Communion and keeping back others." This is closed communion because the altar is not open to just anyone, nor it is open to all who profess to be Christian but only certain Christians.

The sermon Melanchthon has is mind is *Sermon 82* on Matthew 26:26-28. Chrysostom's description of the priest's duties in administering the Lord's body and blood is helpful to read in its entirety. He says:

> 6. These things I say to you that receive, and to you that minister. For it is necessary to address myself to you also, that you may with much care distribute the gifts there. There is no small punishment for you, if being conscious

of any wickedness in any man, you allow him to partake of this table. "His blood shall be required at your hands." Though any one be a general, though a deputy, though it be he himself who is invested with the diadem, and come unworthily, forbid him, the authority thou hast is greater than his. Thou, if thou wert entrusted to keep a spring of water clean for a flock, and then wert to see a sheep having much mire on its mouth, thou wouldest not suffer it to stoop down unto it and foul the stream: but now being entrusted with a spring not of water, but of blood and of spirit, if thou seest any having on them sin, which is more grievous than earth and mire, coming unto it, art thou not displeased? dost thou not drive them off? and what excuse canst thou have?

For this end God hath honored you with this honor, that ye should discern these things. This is your office, this your safety, this your whole crown, not that ye should go about clothed in a white and shining vestment. And whence know I, you may say, this person, and that person? I speak not of the unknown, but of the notorious.

Shall I say something more fearful. It is not so grievous a thing for the energumens [demoniacs] to be within, as for such as these, whom Paul affirms to trample Christ under foot, and to "account the blood of the covenant unclean, and to do despite to the grace of the Spirit." For he that hath fallen into sin and draws nigh, is worse than one possessed with a devil. For they, because they are possessed are not punished, but those, when they draw nigh unworthily, are delivered over to undying punishment. Let us not therefore drive away these only, but all without exception, whomsoever we may see coming unworthily.

Let no one communicate who is not of the disciples. Let no Judas receive, lest he suffer the fate of Judas. This multitude also is Christ's body. Take heed, therefore, thou that ministerest at the mysteries, lest thou provoke the Lord, not purging this body. Give not a sword instead of meat.

Nay, though it be from ignorance that he come to communicate, forbid him, be not afraid. Fear God, not man. If thou shouldest fear man, thou wilt be laughed to scorn even by him, but if God, thou wilt be an object of respect even to men.

But if thou darest not to do it thyself, bring him to me; I will not allow any to dare do these things. I would give up my life rather than impart of the Lord's blood to the unworthy; and will shed my own blood rather than impart of such awful blood contrary to what is meet.

But if any hath not known the bad man, after much inquiry, it is no blame. For these things have been said about the open sinners. For if we amend these, God will speedily discover to us the unknown also; but if we let these alone, wherefore should He then make manifest those that are hidden.

But these things I say, not that we repel them only, nor cut them off, but in order that we may amend them, and bring them back, that we may take care of them. For thus shall we both have God propitious, and shall find many to receive worthily; and for our own diligence, and for our care for others, receive great reward; unto which God grant we may all attain by the grace and love towards man of our Lord Jesus Christ, to whom be glory world without end. Amen.[33]

---

[33] NPNF[1] 10:477-478

There are two types of Christians who are not to be admitted to the Lord's Supper. The first is the notorious sinner. By this Chrysostom means someone whose sin is publicly known. The second is the ignorant.

John Chrysostom described the priest's responsibility in the late 4th century. Justin Martyr, who died around 165, describes the same practice in mid-second century Rome and sheds light on what Chrysostom means by "the ignorant." Justin writes:

> And this food is called among us Εὐχαριστία [the Eucharist], of which no one is allowed to partake but the man who believes that the things which we teach are true, and who has been washed with the washing that is for the remission of sins, and unto regeneration, and who is so living as Christ has enjoined.[34]

According to Justin there are three requirements. The first requirement is unity in belief. The communicant "believes that the things which we teach are true." By this Justin means more than simply the doctrine of Christ's real presence in the Lord's Supper, though that is certainly included. He means the entire Christian faith. So the first requirement to commune at the altar is agreement with the doctrine taught at that particular altar. The second requirement is baptism. The third requirement is a Christian life. The communicant isn't living in manifest, public sin. The unbaptized, the publicly known sinner, and those ignorant of the Christian doctrine are not to be admitted to the Lord's Supper.

This is a reflection of St. Luke's testimony in Acts 2:42 that the Christians "continued steadfastly in the apostles' doctrine and fellowship, in the breaking of bread, and in prayers." Unity in the apostles' doctrine was integral for worship and receiving the Lord's Supper.

---

[34] *First Apology*, 66. (ANF 1:185)

Lutherans confess this practice of closed communion in the *Apology of the Augsburg Confession.* "For among us masses are celebrated every Lord's Day and on the other festivals, in which the Sacrament is offered to those who wish to use it, after they have been examined and absolved" (Ap XXIV.1). Communicants are examined to make sure they hold to the apostles' doctrine. They are absolved in confession so that they understand the Sacrament is for the forgiveness of sins and the strengthening of their God-given faith. If the pastor hasn't examined potential communicants he shouldn't commune them.

What about visitors from other Lutheran congregations? This is where church fellowship comes in. Are they in fellowship with your pastor? Is there doctrinal agreement between your pastor and theirs? In our day that's expressed in church fellowship. So do the visitors belong to a congregation that's part of your pastor's doctrinal fellowship? If not, then they have no business communing, not because they don't believe in Christ's real presence, but because they are not united with your congregation in the apostles' doctrine. Church membership is, after all, a public confession of one's faith, just as important as one's verbal confession of private belief.

This too, is addressed in the early church. The fourth century *Apostolic Constitutions* states, "The deacon shall immediately say, Let none of the catechumens, let none of the hearers, let none of the unbelievers, let none of the heterodox, stay here."[35] The heterodox were Christians of different confessions, who were not in communion with the local bishop and congregation.

Closed Communion prevents people who don't believe Christ's words from eating and drinking to their own judgment. It also confesses that unity in the apostles' doctrine is the Lord's will for His people and a prerequisite for unity at the Lord's Table.

---

[35] Book VII.12.2 (ANF 7:486)

Reservation of the Sacrament

Q: Hi pastor, I wanted to ask you for your opinion on the reservation of the Sacrament and the use of things like tabernacles for this purpose, I had seen it primarily in Romanist churches and Anglo-Catholic congregations but recently I have seen it in some Lutheran churches, mostly LCMS. If it is not done for the worship of the elements, is it a legitimate practice or do you have another opinion on this.

A: I'm aware of Lutheran pastors reserving consecrated elements in tabernacles. It's my understanding that the reserved elements are taken, later in the week, to the sick and shut-in, or used during the next celebration of the Lord's Supper. The rationale for reserving the host in a tabernacle is the belief that Christ's sacramental presence remains indefinitely in the consecrated elements until those elements are eaten and drunk. Since the Word of the Lord endures forever, any interval of time between the consecration and the distribution and reception of the Lord's Supper is irrelevant. Rather than debating the duration of Christ's sacramental presence, the best way to think about the practice of reservation is to compare it with Christ's institution of the Supper to see whether or not the practice agrees with the institution.

When Christ institutes the Sacrament it is an action that consists of three 'parts.' St. Matthew writes: "Jesus took bread, blessed and broke it, and gave it to the disciples and said, 'Take, eat; this is My body.' Then He took the cup, and gave thanks, and gave it to them, saying, 'Drink from it, all of you. For this is My blood of the new covenant, which is shed for many for the remission of sins'" (Matthew 26:26-28). The first action is the consecration. Jesus takes bread and wine and gives thanks. The second action is distribution. He gives the consecrated bread and wine to them to eat and drink. The third action, reception of the consecrated bread and wine, is assumed in Matthew's text, but Mark explicitly writes in Mark 14:23 that they all drank from it. The sacrament is an action consisting of consecration, distribution, and reception, otherwise known as eating and drinking. Lutherans confess in the *Formula of Concord*:

> But this blessing alone, or the recitation of the words of the institution of Christ constitute no sacrament, if the whole action of this Supper, as it was ordered by Christ, be not observed ; if, for instance, the consecrated bread be not administered, received, and enjoyed, but be locked up, sacrificed, or borne about. But the command of Christ, this do, must be observed entire and inviolate, which comprises the whole action or administration of this sacrament ; namely, in a Christian assembly, to take bread and wine, to bless, to administer, and to receive them, that is, to eat and to drink, and at the same time to show the death of the Lord, as also St. Paul presents before our eyes the whole action of breaking bread, or of distributing it and receiving it, 1 Cor. 10:16–17. (FC SD VII.84)

All three actions must be done in order to celebrate the Sacrament in the way Christ instituted it. If all three actions aren't observed, there is no Sacrament. When the Roman Church consecrates bread, encloses in a Monstrance and parades it about or lets people adore it, she is replacing distribution and reception with different actions. Therefore what's being adored at Eucharistic Adoration or the Corpus Christi procession isn't Christ's body. Those actions are outside the sacramental actions Christ instituted.

When a Lutheran pastor reserves the Sacrament in a tabernacle, it isn't for the purpose of adoration or to parade it around. It's usually for the purpose of taking communion to the sick, hospitalized, and shut-in throughout the week.

Martin Chemnitz argued that the Sacrament shouldn't be reserved under any circumstances because reservation separates the sacramental action. He writes in the *Examination of the Council of Trent*:

> The matter is not obscure if we set before ourselves as norm and rule the description of the institution. For Christ first of all used His words, which He wanted to have come to the element in order that it might become a sacrament; He used them in the place and at the time where and when He was about to distribute Communion, and in the presence of those to whom He wanted to communicate His body and blood. Therefore it agrees better with the description of the institution and the example of Christ to recite the words of institution and by means of them to bless the Eucharist at the place and time of Communion, in the presence of those who are to be communed, rather than at another place and time in the absence of those to whom it was to be offered.[36]

Christ instituted the Sacrament at the time when and the place where He was going to distribute it and the disciples were going to eat and drink it. Chemnitz also states that the words, "Take, eat," and "Do this," aren't directed at the elements, but to those who were about to commune. "Therefore," he writes, "it is not in accord with the institution to direct these words only to the bread and wine, and that in the absence of those who are to be communed."[37] Elsewhere He writes that it is the Papists who constructed the idea that by virtue of the words of institution Christ is compelled to remain in the bread and wine with His

---

[36] Martin Chemnitz, *Examination of the Council of Trent*, Vol. 2, 311.
[37] Ibid.

body and blood in an enduring union even for days, months, or even years.[38] Reservation is unacceptable because it separates the sacramental action. Johann Gerhard notes that Jesus didn't delay for a lengthy period of time before distributing the supper to his disciples when he writes, "Accordingly, if it is to be called the Lord's Supper, the distribution is to take place shortly after the blessing or consecration, and the distribution is to be shortly followed by the communicants' eating of the consecrated and distributed bread."[39]

Since reservation separates the sacramental action it needs to be avoided. The best practice is for the minister to consume the reliqua—that is, any remaining consecrated elements—after everyone has communed. This way the sacramental action— consecration, distribution, and reception—is observed as Christ commanded. This was Luther's counsel to Simon Wolferinus in 1543. He wrote, "For you can do what we do here [in Wittenberg], namely, to eat and drink the remains of the Sacrament with the communicants, so that it is not necessary to raise these scandalous and dangerous questions about when the action of the Sacrament ends, questions in which you will choke unless you come to your senses."[40] The celebrant and any other pastors should reverently consume the reliqua since Christ said "Take, eat; Take, drink." This cuts off all speculation by doing what Christ commands to be done. When the pastor takes communion to the sick he consecrates bread and wine in the person's home, in their hearing. All of this agrees much better with Christ's institution than reserving the Sacrament, which only introduces more questions than it answers.

---

[38] Ibid., 249.

[39] Gerhard, *Comprehensive Explanation*, 350.

[40] Martin Luther, [First] Letter to Simon Wolferinus [1543], in Edward Frederick Peters, *The Origin and Meaning of the Axiom: "Nothing Has the Character of a Sacrament Outside of the Use,"* 207-08.

Can Christians Commune Themselves?

Q: Dear Pastor, What can a person do to take communion when there is not a church within any reasonable driving distance? Can I give myself communion after my self-examination and use wine and read the words (which I know by heart) of the Lord's Supper?

A: Whenever we talk about the Lord's Supper we must always deal with it as it has been instituted by Christ. Self-communion violates Christ's institution of the Sacrament in that it separates the Lord's Supper from the Church.

When Christ instituted the Sacrament of the Altar, He gave it to the church, not to individuals for private use. Self-Communion takes the Lord's Supper, given to the Church, and uses it for one's private devotion. Luther speaks against communing oneself in the *Smalcald Articles*. He writes:

> And if any one, for the purpose of making a pious appearance, should pretend that he would, as a devotional exercise, give or administer the Lord's Supper to himself, there could be no sincerity in this ; for if he had a sincere desire to commune, it could be administered to him best and most appropriately in the Sacrament, according to the institution of Christ. But for a person to administer the Sacrament to himself, is a human presumption, uncertain and unnecessary, as well as forbidden.

> Neither does he know what he is doing, since, without the Word of God, he follows false conceptions and fantasies of men. Nor would it be right, if all else were unexceptionable, for one to use the common Sacrament of the church according to his own caprice, and to sport with it at his pleasure, independently of the Word of God, and apart from the communion of the church. (SA II.II.8-9)

Communion is a communal act for the church. Communing oneself takes it away from the church and makes it into an individualistic act. As Luther points out, it is a violation of the Christ's institution of the Sacrament and a human invention. Even when the Lord's Supper is taken to individual shut-in members of a parish it is still a) done by the called pastor and b) it is still done as the church's Sacrament.

Self-communion violates the institution of Christ further in that it separates the Sacrament of Christ from the servants of Christ. On the night in which Christ was betrayed He administered the Sacrament to His disciples. Christ is still the one who administers and distributes His true body and blood to penitent Christians whenever the Lord's Supper is celebrated. He doesn't do it without the use of an intermediary like He did on the night in which He was betrayed. He administers His body and blood through His called and ordained servants. The original Lord's Supper He celebrated "immediately" while every subsequent celebration of the Lord's Supper He administers "mediately," that is, through the hands of His pastors.

Paul says of himself and his fellow ministers in 1 Corinthians 3:9, "We are God's fellow workers." In 1 Corinthians 4:1 he writes, "Let a man so consider us, as servants of Christ and stewards of the mysteries of God." By "mysteries" he means the preaching of the gospel and the administration of the Sacraments. He describes pastors as "stewards of God" again in Titus 1:7. The New Testament ties the administration of the Lord's Supper to the Pastoral Office, just as it ties preaching and the administration of Holy Baptism to the Pastor Office. Christ works through His called and ordained servants. So to take the matter into your own hands in your own home takes Christ's Sacraments away from Christ's stewards, whom He has called and ordained to do just that.

Unlike Baptism, which is necessary for salvation, so that in the case of a true emergency a layman can do it, there is no such thing as "emergency" Lord's Supper. The oral eating of Christ's true body and blood isn't required for salvation in the Scriptures, whereas baptism is. Baptizing, absolving, preaching, and administering the Sacrament, all these mysteries of Christ are done by Christ Himself through His stewards, His pastors. This doesn't mean that pastors have an "indelible mark" or special power to bring about the consecration in and of themselves. It's about the institution of Christ, who gave the Sacrament to His Church, and administers it Himself through His called and ordained servants. Since self-communion violates Christ's institution, we ought to stay away from the practice.

Now that's what you *shouldn't* do. How about what you *should* do? If you find yourself separated from a faithful pastor and parish by a great distance or physical disability, you have two options.

The first is to simply go without the Lord's Supper. Take comfort in the fact that the oral eating of Christ's true body and blood, while a comforting means of grace, is not necessary for salvation. The spiritual eating of Christ, which is simply faith in the words and promises of Christ, is sufficient for your soul. You spiritually eat of Christ whenever you read the Scriptures and apply those promises to yourself, or when you hear sermons preached online and do the same. As Christians we have to uphold Christ's institution of the Lord's Supper. If you have to abstain from the Sacrament, think of that as a cross for you to bear. Don't try to find a way to unload your cross, but bear it patiently, trusting Christ.

The second thing you should do is contact the nearest faithful pastor and speak to him about the possibility of joining his congregation from a distance. There is a definite possibility that he will be able to close the distance and find a way to serve you with God's word and Sacraments. Back in the old days of the American frontier, pastors were circuit riders, traveling around their area to multiple points where there were people who desired faithful Word and Sacrament ministry.

As our culture becomes increasingly paganized and the visible church slides further into indifference and apostasy, the old model of circuit riding pastors is necessary once again. The Lord provided for His faithful Christians back then through His called and ordained servants, He will provide for you now as well.

Can Elders Give Communion to Shut-Ins?

Q: My church is large enough that we typically have 15-20 shut-ins at any given time. That's too many people for the Pastor to visit all of them on a weekly or even a monthly basis for a small in-home church service, including Communion. So to help, the Elders typically do these in-home services and serve Communion. Do you think its okay for Elders to serve Communion in cases like this?

A: I assume by "Elder" you mean a lay leader in the congregation. I say this because in the New Testament the word translated "Elder" is πρεσβύτερος, which is typically a man who holds the Office of the Ministry. In our language today a πρεσβύτερος is a pastor. "Lay-elders" seem to be a uniquely American Lutheran phenomenon. For the sake of not adding to the confusion, I'll call them laymen, since that's what they are.

So should laymen be serving communion to shut-ins in their homes? You don't give any specifics on how this is being done so I'll address both ways that this might be happening. The first option is that the layman is consecrating the elements in the shut-in's home during a brief service. If this is happening it needs to stop immediately. Lutherans confess in the fourteenth article of the Augsburg Confession, "Of Ecclesiastical Order they teach that no one should publicly teach in the Church or administer the Sacraments unless he be regularly called." We confess this because the Scriptures teach it. Paul calls himself and his fellow ministers, "servants of Christ and stewards of the mysteries of God" in 1 Corinthians 4:1.

Lutherans confess in the *Apology of the Augsburg Confess* that the "mysteries of God" are the "Gospel and the sacraments" (Ap XXIV.80). Paul also says in Romans 10:15, "How shall they preach unless they are sent?" The question isn't about preaching but this is relevant to the topic. God has given the responsibility of stewarding and administering the Gospel and sacraments to the Office of the Ministry. When a laymen consecrates the elements and celebrates the Lord's Supper, that celebration isn't being done according to Christ's institution since the Scripture assigns the administration of the Sacrament to the pastoral office.

Something else to consider is that celebrating a brief communion service in a shut-in's home will involve preaching. This also belongs to the pastoral office, which is why I brought up the Romans 10:15 passage. Laymen aren't to preach in the church. That means more than "in the church building." It means only those whom God has called and ordained should be preaching to the church, whether it means in the church building, in a park, at a hospital bedside, or a homebound member's living room. A practical consideration, too, is that a pastor's homily to a homebound member often adjusts to some extent to the member's circumstances. There have been times when I've entered a home and had to preach something entirely different than I intended because of health or family developments.

The second option is that the pastor consecrates elements during the Divine Service, which are then set aside to be given to the layman, who then takes them to the shut-in. I'm familiar with one Missouri Synod church in which the pastor reserves some of the elements and after everyone has communed, he places them in a box and hands them to a woman who is in charge of distributing them to the homebound.

Reserving some of the elements to be taken to the sick and shut-in isn't a good practice. It contradicts Christ's institution by separating the sacramental action. The sacramental action consists of consecration, distribution, and reception, by which we mean eating and drinking. Reserving some of the consecrated elements to be distributed and received at a later time tears the eating and drinking apart from the consecration.

Martin Chemnitz addresses this issue in volume two of his Examination of the Council of Trent. He writes:

> The matter is not obscure if we set before ourselves as norm and rule the description of the institution. For Christ first of all used His words, which He wanted to have come to the element in order that it might become a sacrament; He used them in the place and at the time where and when He was about to distribute Communion, and in the presence of those to whom He wanted to communicate His body and blood. Therefore it agrees better with the description of the institution and the example of Christ to recite the words of institution and by means of them to bless the Eucharist at the place and time of Communion, in the presence of those who are to be communed, rather than at another place and time in the absence of those to whom it was to be offered.[41]

Christ used His words, which instituted the Sacrament, in the place and at the time where and when he was going to distribute it. He also said the words of institution in the presence of those to whom He was distributing His body and blood. His point is that there was no reservation of elements to be reserved for a later time by people who weren't physically present. He goes on to make the point that the words, "Take, eat," and "Do this," aren't directed at the elements, but to those who were about to commune. He says, "Therefore it is not in accord with the institution to direct these words only to the bread and wine, and that in the absence of those who are to be communed."[42] Chemnitz goes on to make several other points,

---

[41] Martin Chemnitz, *Examination of the Council of Trent*, Vol. 2, 311.
[42] Ibid.

one of which is that since the benefit of the Supper is necessary most of all for the sick, it's right that the words of institution be recited in the presence and hearing of the sick person.

Then he writes, "For these reasons our men, in the Communion of the sick, recite the words of the Supper, which are in fact the consecration, in the presence of the sick person."[43] This isn't the recitation of the Words of Institution over elements which have been previously consecrated, because he writes that the recitation of the words "are in fact the consecration." Clearly, pastors celebrated the Lord's Supper in the homes of the sick. Those who were to be communed were present for the words of institution, so that the sacramental action was held together.

In the case of fifteen to twenty shut-ins at any given time, the best thing to do would be for the church to call a second pastor. If that's not an option then a different shut-in schedule needs to be worked out. Perhaps the shut-ins don't receive the Lord's Supper as often as they'd like. While that's not ideal it's better than the uncertainty of a lay consecration or tearing the distribution and reception away from the consecration.

Christ has assigned the celebration of the Lord's Supper to His called and ordained stewards. It's up to your pastor to find a faithful way to make that happen with that many shut-ins. To make sure they're getting the Word of God, mail the weekly service bulletin and sermon to each one of them. It would also be helpful for him to remind everyone in the flock what Gerhard says about these things, "Where one cannot have access to an ordained pastor, the spiritual reception of the body and blood of Christ is adequate for salvation if one cannot obtain the sacramental reception."[44]

---

[43] Ibid., p. 312.
[44] Gerhard, *Comprehensive Explanation*, 226.

Holy Communion and the Legal Drinking Age[45]

Q: I have a question about the Lord's Supper. Since Lutherans use wine wouldn't it be illegal to allow children to partake of the cup since U.S. law says you have to be at least 21 years old to drink alcohol?

A: Legal Disclaimer: I am not a lawyer and nothing in this chapter should be considered legal advice.

Lutherans use wine in the Lord's Supper because that is the element Christ used when He instituted the Sacrament. Does our communing of minors put us at odds with state laws that set a minimum legal drinking age? No. But the answer is complex and takes us to the heart of religious liberty debates.

According to law, the minimum legal drinking age is 21 in every state. But we're dealing with law so it's never as easy as it seems. Forty-five states have specific legal exceptions that allow minors to consume alcohol under certain circumstances. For example, according to Chapter 106 of the Texas Beverage Code, underage consumption of alcohol is allowed "if it is in the presence of the minor's adult parent, guardian, or spouse."[46] Other states are stricter regarding stated exceptions to the minimum legal drinking age; in Missouri, for instance, minors are allowed to taste alcoholic beverages for educational purposes during culinary courses. That being said, about half the states provide statutory regulations allowing minors to drink alcohol for religious purposes. So the question isn't as cut and dried as it may seem.

In those states that don't have explicit religious exemptions for minors or don't allow minors to consume alcohol with parental permission, we would turn to the implicit exemption set forth

---

[45] Special thank Rev. Jeffery Ahonen for his help with this topic.
[46] Title 4 Chapter 106.5

in the free exercise clause in the First Amendment to the United States Constitution. The First Amendment begins: "Congress shall make no law respecting an establishment of religion, or prohibiting the free exercise thereof." This would seem to make a straightforward legal argument to an open-and-shut case on the question of Holy Communion practice. But even that is not the end of the story. While the government cannot regulate religious belief, to compel you to believe or not believe something, it can restrict, under certain circumstances, how that belief is expressed in society.

Several Supreme Court cases throughout America's history have defined to what extent and under what circumstances the government can prohibit religious practices. Importantly, the government can curtail religious practices that violate the moral or social order. For instance, Reynolds vs. U.S. in 1878 ruled that the government could prohibit polygamy because it destroyed social order. Mormons were free to believe that polygamy was an acceptable practice; they just weren't allowed to practice it. Another example following the ruling in the Reynolds case is the Mohammedan who believes that infidels should be exterminated and that honor killings are one's religious duty. They are free to believe those things, but they cannot legally practice them because to do so would violate the moral and statutory law that forbids murder.

Later rulings, like the 1990 federal Supreme Court case *Employment Division, Department of Human Resources v. Smith*, held that religious beliefs can be infringed to ensure compliance with other law beyond law impacting moral and social order. This means that one's religious practice doesn't excuse you from obeying state and federal laws. If the government has a compelling interest, it can prohibit religious practices that conflict with other laws. What is a "compelling interest?" Most often it is an existing statute or a financial government interest.

The Smith case was unpopular, as it was viewed by many as too restrictive upon religious rights, and this led Congress to pass the RFRA, the *Religious Freedom Restoration Act* in 1993. Like the Smith case, the RFRA states that the government can burden someone's religious practice if it has a compelling interest, but, and here's the point of the RFRA, the limitation on free exercise has to be by the "least restrictive means" available.

So what does all this have to do with the minor communicant at a Lutheran altar? In those states that have an explicit religious exemption to the Minimum Legal Drinking Age, the statute sets forth clearly that their partaking is perfectly legal. In Texas, the minor will usually have a parent present with them, and therefore, as the statutory code indicates, communing with a parent present would be permitted. In the states without any specified exemptions for underage alcohol consumption, the free exercise clause in the First Amendment would be used to legally defend the minor's partaking in the Sacrament.

But that's not the end of the matter, either, because the government does have a compelling interest in limiting the consumption of alcohol to minors. The government prohibits minors from drinking for several reasons, one of which is drinking and driving. Of course, in the Sacrament of the Altar the amount of wine the communicant receives is so miniscule that it's not going to lead to intoxication, or mental and emotional impairment. Nevertheless, the government has a compelling interest in the matter because it would endanger lives to have minors driving with alcohol in their system.

Since there is a compelling interest the government could attempt to burden the minor's religious practice by banning their use of sacramental wine altogether. But the RFRA requires "the least restrictive means of furthering that compelling governmental interest." A complete ban on the use of sacramental wine to minors wouldn't be the "least restrictive means" for keeping minors from doing harm to themselves or others while under the influence. If the government's concern is impaired driving by teens, then the least restrictive means is to limit the amount of wine that can be consumed in a religious ceremony. New York State, for instance, does this; it limits the amount of sacramental wine a minor can have to 2 ounces. That law balances the government's compelling interest and the minor's right to freely exercise his religion.

The RFRA protects minors so that they may partake of the Lord's Supper, but it also requires they follow other laws about alcohol use. Since most states ban teens from driving with any amount of alcohol in their systems, minors who partake of the Lord's Supper are required to obey that law. Paul writes in Titus 3:1, "Be subject to rulers and authorities, to obey, to be ready for every good work." The minor communicant should have a ride home from the Divine Service, even though he's not at all intoxicated.

The question at hand, and the entire subject of religious freedom in the United States, is best understood from a two kingdoms perspective. God has placed us in His church and in the world, under earthly authority. Christians can't choose to only live in the realm of the church and snub the earthly authority which God has established. Christ Himself tells us to "render to Caesar the things that are Caesar's, and to God the things that are God's" (Matthew 22:21). The minor renders to God the things that are God's by partaking of the Lord's Supper so that He can have his sins forgiven by receiving the true body and blood Christ. He renders to Caesar obedience and honor by making sure he has a ride home so as to obey the laws of Caesar.

Internet Communion and Disease Transmission

Q: Dear Pastor, how has Covid-19 changed the way you do the Lord's Supper? What do you think about internet communion where a pastor blesses bread and wine over Skype or Zoom? Have you stopped using the common chalice to limit the spread of the virus, or have you stopped celebrating Holy Communion altogether?

A: The Covid-19 pandemic has changed the way most people live to some extent, and the church isn't immune to the change that things like this bring. In those places where there are "stay-at-home" orders, churches aren't able to meet together physically. However, in the internet age, they're able to worship electronically via live streaming services. This is a tremendous blessing not only for nourishing the flock with God's Word but also as a witness to the world. Some pastors have introduced a novelty into the church that needs to be addressed: celebrating the Lord's Supper over the internet.

For those churches that are still able to physically meet together for worship, although in services of no more than five or ten people, the Lord's Supper is still being celebrated in its usual way. That's raised the question of whether or not communicants can catch a virus like Covid-19 by drinking from the chalice which is common to all the communicants. On the one hand there are people who claim it's not a safe practice and individual cups should be used, while on the other hand there are those who claim that because of what the Lord's Supper is there's no way it could communicate sickness between communicants. This episode of ATP addresses these two questions: 1) Can Holy Communion be celebrated over the internet and 2) whether the Chalice is safe to use in times of sickness?

To answer the first question, "No. Holy Communion *cannot* be celebrated over the internet." Any attempt to do so isn't the Lord's Supper but a mockery of the Sacrament. Whenever we're dealing with the issue of whether or not a celebration of the Sacrament is valid, the litmus test is, "Is it being faithful to the sacramental action?" The sacramental action consists of three parts: Consecration, Distribution, and Reception. In "Internet Communion," the elements the pastor consecrates are consecrated, but the Words of Institution don't apply to any and every piece of bread and wine that he doesn't intend for sacramental use. Nor can the pastor intend the consecration for bread and wine which isn't physically there in front of him. The words of institution, whether livestreamed or recorded, don't apply to any bread and wine that the sound of his voice reaches. This would make the words of institution a magical incantation. Nor can laity consecrate the elements in their homes. They are not in Christ's office to do so.

Nor is there any distribution happening in "internet communion" but a "self-administration." Luther condemns self-communion in the Smalcald Articles (III.2.8-9). Self-communion violates Christ's institution because it's done "apart from the communion of the church." The Lord instituted His Supper as a communal, not an individual act. Christ instituted His Sacrament to be administered to Christians through His called and ordained servants in the Office of the Ministry. They are to administer it to Christians, not Christians to themselves. Even when a pastor communes himself during the liturgy he does so because he is part of the congregation. The pastor is also to examine and absolve potential communicants so that Christ's body and blood aren't given to the impenitent or people who believe doctrine other than the apostles' doctrine. Pastoral responsibility can't be exercised in "internet communion."

Since there is no consecration of the elements at one's home, there can be no distribution or reception of the Lord's body and blood. In the case of internet communion, the Lord's Supper is not being celebrated.

Some may argue that this is an "emergency situation" but it's not. Emergencies entail death or dying. Even then, there is no such thing as emergency communion. Emergency baptism is allowable, and encouraged, since baptism is necessary for salvation. The Lord's Supper is not. This situation isn't an emergency. It's an inconvenience that calls for faithfulness to what God has given us, not innovation that blasphemously destroys the good gifts that God has given us.

Regarding the second question, "Is the chalice safe to use during times of sickness?" The typical answer is "Yes, because the wine and the gold, or silver, of the chalice have anti-microbial properties." However, studies have shown that those things don't stop pathogenic organisms. In a review in the *International Journal of Infectious Diseases*, Volume 17 from 2013, James Pellerin and Michael Edmond write:

> In 1967 Hobbs and colleagues performed experiments that concluded that silver and wine may have antimicrobial properties. However, the time interval between each communicants drinking from the cup, which is typically less than five seconds, is not sufficient to cause a significant decrease in bacterial counts. They also found that rotating the chalice was ineffective at decreasing colonization; however wiping the rim with the linen cloth decreased bacterial counts by 90%. All studies concluded that the risk of spreading disease cannot be excluded but is extremely low.[47]

---

[47]   https://www.sciencedirect.com/science/article/pii/S1201971213001872 (Accessed August 25, 2021)

So the antimicrobial properties of wine and the precious metal of the chalice, by themselves, don't make the chalice safe. But when the rim is wiped with a linen cloth after each communicant, the risk of spreading sickness is "extremely low." The authors of the review note:

> Finally, in 1998 the CDC reported there had never been an outbreak of infection related to the communion cup. They referenced a study from 1997 in which 681 participants who drank daily from a common cup were at no higher risk of infection than those who participated less frequently or who completely abstained from Christian services. They concluded that it is probably safe to participate in services where a common cup is used, with the caveat that any member of the congregation with active respiratory illness or open labial or mouth sores abstain from partaking.[48]

According to the CDC there is virtually no risk from using the chalice. However, those who have active respiratory illness or open sores in their or mouth should abstain since there's a possibility of communicating those illnesses to others via the chalice. Communion isn't necessary for salvation so if you're ill with these illnesses you should refrain out of love for your neighbor.

There are some who respond by quoting a phrase from the third stanza of the hymn *What God Ordains is Always Good*,[49] which reads, "No poison can be in the cup that my Physician sends me." Except that stanza isn't about the Lord's Supper. In stanza 5 we sing "What God ordains is always good. Though I the cup am drinking Which savors now of bitterness, I take it without

---

[48] Ibid.
[49] Samuel Rodigast, "What God Ordains Is Always Good" (No. 521) in The Lutheran Hymnal, St. Louis: Concordia Publishing House. 1941.

shrinking. For after grief God grants relief, My heart with comfort filling And all my sorrow stilling." The "cup" is the cup of trial, cross, and suffering, which is why we can sing in stanza six, "Though sorrow, need, or death be mine, I shall not be forsaken." Even if you do catch something from another communicant and die, you're still unharmed because you've trusted in Christ's words and by faith received His gifts He gives in the Supper. Others will cite Ignatius of Antioch's epistle to the Ephesians, chapter 20:2, where Ignatius calls the Lord's Supper "the medicine of immortality, the antidote we take in order not to die but to live forever in Jesus Christ." Ignatius speaks of spiritual life bestowed in the Sacrament, not earthly life and health. This is evident from his words that we take the medicine of immorality "in order not to die but to live forever in Jesus Christ."

While it is possible to spread certain illnesses via the Chalice, the chances of this are very low. The chalice is much more hygienic than plastic or glass individual cups that have been touched by others when they're filled, and have other hands floating around them during the distribution. If you're able to commune during the Covid-19 pandemic, do so without fear. But if you have the symptoms or feel ill, stay home for your own sake and the sake of your fellow saints whom you love.

ABOUT THE AUTHOR

Rev. Joshua Sullivan graduated from Concordia Seminary in St. Louis, Missouri with a Masters of Divinity. He serves as pastor of Holy Cross Lutheran Church in Kerrville, Texas. He and his wife have three children.

Made in the USA
Columbia, SC
28 November 2022

72227607R00054